HEROES&‾ HEROINES

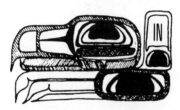

IN

TLINGIT-HAIDA

LEGEND

BY MARY L. BECK

ILLUSTRATED BY NANCY DeWITT

Alaska Northwest Books™

ANCHORAGE • SEATTLE

Second printing 1990

Library of Congress Cataloging-in-Publication Data
Beck, Mary L., 1924-
    Heroes and heroines of Tlingit-Haida legend and their counterparts in classical mythology / by Mary L. Beck; illustrated by Nancy DeWitt.
        p.   cm.
    Bibliography: p.
    ISBN 0-88240-334-6
    1. Haida Indians — Legends. 2. Tlingit Indians — Legends. 3. Mythology, Classical — Cross-cultural studies.   I. Title.
E99.H2B43   1989
398.2'089972—dc20   89-14931
                                                                      CIP

Edited by Ethel Dassow
Cover and book design by Lynn Hamrick
Illustrations by Nancy DeWitt

Alaska Northwest Books™
A division of GTE Discovery Publications, Inc.
22026 20th Avenue S.E.
Bothell, WA 98021

Printed in U.S.A.

To my husband, George

And thanks to my editor and friend, Ethel Dassow

C O N T E N T S

F O R E W O R D

The oral literature of Southeast Alaska Natives, like that of other primitive cultures, evolved from the universal human need to understand and explain how it all began, what forces are in control, how man fits into the scheme of things, how to live in harmony with the natural forces and the other creatures of the earth — some of which man must kill if he is to survive — and to transmit these concepts to posterity.

The literature deals with significant events in tribal, clan or family history, with adventures and misadventures of folk heroes, with supernatural forces, and with relationships and interchanges between human and nonhuman beings.

Some myths and legends had their origins in a past so distant that no one knows what seeds they grew from. Others are relatively recent. They are neither all fact nor all fantasy. They are allegories, parables, metaphoric presentations of cultural values and the socially accepted life view.

Nature is so bountiful in Southeast Alaska that its aborigines had leisure to develop a complex culture, which survives in their unique and sophisticated graphic arts, their music and dances and their rich oral literature.

The myths and legends were told and retold at potlatches, less formal gatherings, as family pastimes, even as bedtime stories. But their entertainment value was secondary. Here, as elsewhere, the important function of myth and legend was to pass the knowledge of traditions, morals and mores from the old to the young, maintain social cohesion and continuity, keep the culture alive and flourishing.

Even today, though these people have been literate for generations and have entered mainstream culture, they keep the art of storytelling alive.

To the Tlingits and Haidas the oral literature of the lineage, the clan or the tribe is hereditary property, intangible but nonetheless owned. As a group grew, divided and subdivided, none relinquished ownership of the group's intangible properties. In time, some related groups were separated by hundreds of miles of waterways and islands, and mutual ownership of intangible properties served as a bond of kinship.

With tribal intermarriage, some intangible properties passed into shared ownership. Or they might be transmitted as gifts or spoils of battle, in trade or as ransom. Thus the stories of the Tlingits and the Haidas, their music and dances and their visual symbols have much in common.

Just as language itself evolves over time, the oral literature evolved as a detail was added here or subtracted there, a name was remembered differently or deliberately changed, emphasis was altered, and so there were several versions of most stories before any were recorded.

The myths and legends collected here are authentic for one group or another, though other versions may be equally authentic.

Names of the heroes and heroines are usually omitted to avoid confusion or encroachment upon private property. The stories in themselves are worth telling, and in their parallels to the myths and legends of other cultures, they reinforce the one-world concept. Through them we see that human needs, reactions and values are essentially the same everywhere, and that human beings, wherever they live, have found similar ways of explaining life and transmitting their concepts.

Ethel Dassow
April 1989

P R E F A C E

Inside the large community house, its plank walls painted with ancestral crest figures, the people gather around the central fireplace according to rank and social status. They have come for a potlatch. The host group presides over the festivities. Maybe they have gathered to proclaim a new chief or honor a passing one. Or they might want to formalize claims to a clan crest or celebrate the taking of a new name by a young man come of age. Whatever the occasion, many gifts will be given, and it will be a time of feasting, singing and dancing, of honoring lineages and of telling ancestral stories.

Some of these stories, passed on orally through the years, belong to individual groups, the only ones entitled to tell them. But others are clan stories, so popular they have been told in different ways by many groups who honor the same heroes as part of their heritage. This is true of the story of Natsilane, the skilled carver who fashioned the mighty Killer Whale from cedar and coaxed it into life. Other widely claimed clan legends include the story of Gunarh, who dared to invade the underworld and snatch his wife back to earth, and the tale of Blackskin's bare-handed struggle with sea lions to avenge his uncle's death. In fact, the figure of Blackskin tearing the huge sea lion in half is carved on the cedar posts of this community house.

Heroes did not usually inherit their special powers. They had to prove worthy first by obeying clan codes and bathing in icy water, fasting, and exercising strenuously. Devotion to the crest animals, who often gave them their special powers, was important too. The Boy Who Fed Eagles gained honor, wealth and power for having shown respect to eagles in spite of his family's disapproval. It was while making his preparations in secret that the young man who became Gonakadet was inspired with a plan for trapping the luck-bearing monster. Then by wearing the monster's skin, he was able to provide his starving village with food.

The heroines of these myths sometimes bring good fortune and sometimes do not. Rhipsunt married a Bear and bore children who had special hunting powers, which they took with them to her clan. Fog Woman brought salmon to the streams. Creek Woman is the source of all streams. But the same character as Volcano Woman brought destruction to a village, as did the Girl with a Woodworm pet that grew into a monster and devoured the village provisions.

In these stories, regard for clan values is usually rewarded and neglect of them, punished. The deceit of Gonakadet's mother-in-law, the arrogance of Blackskin's cousins and the treachery of Natsilane's brothers-in-law all bring death. The people who neglect the Eagle almost starve, and the kidnappers of Gunarh's wife are subjected to trickery.

Characters of Native lore are often more than just heroes to the individuals who honor them as totems. They are spirit helpers who guide and inspire them and help them develop strength, skills and judgment.

Natsilane and the Killer Whale are clan emblems of Chief Shakes IX of the Nanyaayi of Wrangell and appear on a pole in front of his home in Ketchikan, Alaska. Chief Shakes is Jonathan DeWitt, a

Tlingit Eagle, one of the two phratries (or subdivisions) of the Tlingit tribe, and the husband of the illustrator of these stories, Nancy DeWitt. Jonathan had the pole carved by his father, the late Forrest DeWitt, a noted historian, storyteller, and carver and himself a chief of the Dog Salmon clan of the Raven phratry, the other Tlingit subdivision. The most prominent of the present chief's forebears was Shakes V, who was chief of the Nanyaayi, the ruling clan of Wrangell, when the Russians came to build the Redoubt of St. Dionysius in 1833, and when the British built Fort Stikine during the period of their lease. He was still chief when the United States bought Alaska and built Fort Wrangell, and until his death in 1878.

Since the Killer Whale was then and is still the clan emblem, the Killer Whale story is an important part of the present Chief Shakes's family tradition and has been told over and over at family and clan gatherings. As a child, Jonathan grew up hearing about Natsilane's skill and precision and his influence upon his young brother-in-law. In the storyteller's dramatization of the story, listeners were kept in suspense about whether Natsilane would be saved and the wrongdoers punished.

The Eagle sits on top of the Shakes pole as the phratry symbol, and figures from other family stories also appear. But the story of Natsilane and the Killer Whale holds the warmest place in their hearts.

As we read about the heroes and heroines of Native lore, we realize that they have traits which all cultures admire. Physical strength and skill, cunning and daring, regard for family and community—these are also the qualities of Olympic medalists, space pioneers, Nobel prize-winners and heroes of any society. Readers of any culture should enjoy these stories of heroism and adventure.

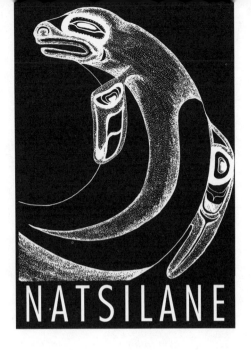

NATSILANE

The life and exploits of Natsilane parallel in some ways those of the Greek Hephaestus. Though his physical skills alone merit hero status, Natsilane is most highly honored as the artisan who created and breathed life into the first Killer Whale (Blackfish). Hephaestus, god of fire (from whom Prometheus stole fire for mankind), is renowned as the first metallurgist, who not only fashioned the glorious shield of Achilles, but also animated the golden handmaidens who served him on Olympus.

Both heroes knew rejection before they

won honor. Hephaestus, cast out as an infant because he was lame, was received by the sea goddesses Eurynome and Thetis and eventually restored to the citadel of the gods. Natsilane's adult brothers-in-law, jealous of his competence, left him on Sea Lion Rock to die. The Sea Lion People took him to their home under the sea floor, then returned him to his village.

Hephaestus became the protector of artisans. Though Natsilane never returned to village life, his Killer Whale, after wreaking vengeance upon the brothers-in-law, became a benefactor to his people.

The Natsilane story is probably the most popular of the Tlingit and Haida myths today, perhaps because many lineages claim the Killer Whale crest. Even today the Killer Whale is said to bring success and wealth to those who see it.

Natsilane was a Tlingit who lived in Southeast Alaska many, many years ago — before there were any killer whales, say those who know. When he took as wife the daughter of a chief on Duke Island, he chose to live among her people instead of taking her back to his own home, as was the custom.

He was from Kake, about two hundred miles to the north, and not much was known about him in the Duke Island village. But his fine build, agile movements and dignified manner hinted that he was of high caste. He was a highly skilled carver, and all the hunters sought him out to carve their spears. He was also an able sea-lion hunter and he won honor in the village for providing this much-loved food. It was not surprising, then, that he should eventually accomplish remarkable things for the village, for he seemed called to greatness.

But he had great obstacles to overcome. A newcomer to the village, he felt that he had to prove himself. To win the respect of his in-laws he tried to be the best in everything he did. He was always first to jump onto the rocks on the sea-lion hunts and he managed to kill most of the sea lions. But his desire to please succeeded only in annoying the older of his brothers-in-law. The youngest of them idolized Natsilane and tried to warn him of his brothers' jealousy. He was watching anxiously as Natsilane carved a spear from a piece of yellow cedar.

"Will it be done in time for the hunt?" he asked. He had just passed his fifteenth birthday and this time he was going to be allowed to try his luck at spearing a sea lion. In the past he had gone along only to help man the boat. But he had always watched closely, seeing how the men jumped quickly from the boat to take the sea lions by surprise.

"It's nearly ready," Natsilane answered. "We can try it out after we bathe." They headed toward the beach.

"My brothers don't like it that you kill so many sea lions," the boy said.

"Oh, a little competition is good," he assured the boy. "It makes us all better hunters." Natsilane had noticed their annoyance, but felt he could win them over.

The two went to sit with the other hunters in the icy water, as all the young men did to gain strength and build resistance to cold. The boy generally got out earlier than the others, since his smaller body chilled through faster than the older men's. But Natsilane was always the last out. Often the men would taunt him for this.

"Why do you have to be the last out all the time?" the oldest brother-in-law asked. "Are you trying to show the rest of us up?"

It was true that Natsilane was trying to show his strength, but it was to win their approval, not to outdo them. He was also used to rigorous training and was competing with himself, trying to stay in the water a little longer each day. He didn't know how to explain this without seeming to brag.

"Come on, Little Brother, let's switch each other," the oldest brother called. He didn't like the younger brother's wide-eyed admiration of Natsilane, and he lashed harder than he should have. Though the switching stung so much it brought tears to his eyes, the young boy did not let on how much it hurt.

"Hah! Your tender flesh is bleeding. You're going to have to toughen some more before the hunt," the older brother scoffed. The boy went down into the water again to wash off and let the sea water heal the open welts. When the others had gone, he spoke to Natsilane.

"My brothers don't like it that you are always the first off the boat to get the sea lions."

"I don't try to outshine them. I just can't help myself," Natsilane answered."My blood rushes when I see large sea lions." His eyes shone at the thought of them. "Our people were great hunters. My uncle trained me well."

"They say you are showing off when you jump from the boat onto the rocks from such great distances."

"You have to move quickly so the boat doesn't hit the rocks. Besides, you have to take the sea lions by surprise. If they see the boat or the hunters, they slip into the water and dive under."

"Couldn't you leave some sea lions for them to kill?"

"The sea lions scramble for water as soon as they know you are there. You have to kill them as fast as you can, once you start." Natsilane was now out of the water and the boy began to lash him with switches.

"Be careful, Natsilane. They can be mean. You saw how hard they switched me."

Natsilane had noticed the sharp lashes and the sneer on the older brother's face, but he did not want to encourage the boy's fears.

"They are probably anxious for you to develop into a man. But they should switch only enough to make the blood tingle. Welts might leave scars. Soon your skin will toughen, though."

"Do you think I will kill a sea lion, Natsilane?"

"Maybe. You have trained well, and you are quick. You are also strong for one so young. Choose a small sea lion and thrust the spear sure and deep. The secret is to leap off the boat onto the rock on the steep side. The sea lions usually sleep on the gentler slope."

"Will I ever hunt as well as you? You are the best."

"Some day you may be better." He smiled as he kneaded the back of the boy's neck in playful roughness. "Come on. Let's go try your spear for size." Natsilane always considered a man's height and arm length when he made spears.

They walked up the beach to the carving shed. The boy picked up the spear and, holding it high over his head, pretended to strike. The weapon seemed a part of his body and he wielded it with natural grace.

"A perfect fit," the carver said. "How does it feel?"

"Just right. It's not heavy or clumsy like my brothers'."

"No. It is the right weight for you."

"My brothers say that you have a magic spear. That is why you kill so many sea lions."

Natsilane laughed. "It's just that I keep shaping the spear to handle right for me. Everyone has to do that for himself. I can't judge so carefully for somebody else as for myself. After you use a spear a little, you will get to know what needs to be done to make it work better for you."

The day of the big sea lion hunt finally came. The men paddled the open canoe toward West Devil Rock, out in the open straits. Natsilane and the four brothers took their turns rowing. The sun was shining overhead, but fog still hung around the rocks and inlets. There was the usual feverish excitement of the hunt. As they got close to the rocks, the older brothers began to look at one another apprehensively. The wind was from the northwest, causing whitecaps on the water and waves to break over the rocks. Natsilane crouched in the bow of the boat, spear in hand, poised to leap.

"Let's get out of here," cried one of the brothers. "The water's too rough. The boat will break on the rocks."

But Natsilane made a giant leap as the boat washed close to the highest point, and he landed face down on the side of the rock. He pulled himself up to the top of the rock where his spear was balanced. Ignoring his bleeding hands, he thrust his spear into the nearest sea lion. But it was a huge one and it tore away, the point of Natsilane's spear stuck in its side.

Natsilane looked about for the canoe and finally spotted it in the distance, pulling farther and farther away. He could see the youngest brother in the stern and heard him calling out, "Go back for him! Go back for him!" But the oarsmen kept going ahead.

The boy called over and over and struggled to get the paddles from them, until one of the brothers pulled him down. "Stay still or you'll capsize the boat. It's too dangerous to go back."

"He can swim out to the boat from the side of the rock away from the wind," the boy said.

"We'll come back for him when the wind dies down." But the brothers had no intention of coming back. They had planned to desert him and tell the villagers he had drowned. By now he probably had, they told themselves, or he had been crushed against the rocks.

In the meantime Natsilane found himself without a spear or food or water. As the afternoon wore

on, he became cold and hungry. But most of all he felt
betrayed. He couldn't believe the brothers-in-law would
leave him there to die. He knew they resented his skill
at hunting, but he was only trying to please them.
Maybe they had heard him and his wife arguing in the
evenings. Didn't they know those were just lovers'
quarrels? They always made up afterward. Maybe the
men were going into a cove for shelter and would pick
him up in the morning. He pulled his cloak up over his
head and fell asleep.

At dawn he was wakened by somebody
calling his name. He sat upright.

"My brothers-in-law have come back for me,"
he thought. He looked in all directions, but saw no one.
The fog hanging over the rock chilled him. He covered
his head and drifted off to sleep again. It was full
daylight when he was again awakened by somebody
calling his name. Through the thick fog Natsilane was
finally able to make out a sea lion that looked like a
man, beckoning to him.

"Come. The chief of the sea lions wants to
see you."

Natsilane was surprised but curious, so
followed the sea lion at a little distance to an opening in
the rock.

"We are now going down into the Sea-Lions'
House," his guide announced.

Natsilane figured he couldn't be much worse
off down there, and maybe it would be warmer than on
the rock. They went down a steep, dark passage and
then came into a large room lighted by a fireplace in
the center.

Around it sat the chief and other sea lions,
warming themselves. They looked like people. The
guide presented him to the chief.

"Welcome to our home, greatest of sea-lion
hunters," the chief said. "Come close to the fire and

warm yourself." He turned to his servant and said, "Get our guest something warm to drink." And then he addressed Natsilane again, "I ask a favor of you. Can you take this thing out that makes my son so sick?"

He took Natsilane to a sick sea lion, which had a medicine man working over him with little success. As Natsilane moved closer, he recognized the sick one as the sea lion he had speared. His own broken spear point was still in the flesh, causing it to be infected. Natsilane bent over the wounded animal and worked his fingers into the swollen flesh until he could get hold of one end of the spear point. With one finger he was able to move the tip back and forth a little, gradually loosening it in the flesh. Then he gripped the end with the tips of his fingers and pulled it free. The infected matter oozed out.

The sea lion seemed relieved of pain and soon fell into a deep sleep. By the next morning the wound had healed greatly and it was almost certain that the sea lion would live.

"We owe much to you, greatest of hunters," said the Sea-Lion Chief. "From now on our spirits will always be with you and will bring you even greater skills. But now we know you are thinking of going home."

He ordered the others to blow up a dried sea-lion stomach and place Natsilane inside so he would drift safely to shore. They pulled the opening together from outside, telling Natsilane to lace it tightly from the inside.

"Think hard of the fine, sandy beach of your village. Do not think of us or of this place," the chief said to him.

Natsilane did as the chief told him. He thought of the sandy beach in front of the village, and of the houses in the trees. What was his young wife doing now? Had the brothers returned yet? What was their story to the village? But then his mind would wander back to the Sea-Lions' House, and he would feel his craft change course and start toward the rock again. He would have to concentrate harder on home and family. It hurt him to think of the brothers-in-law. How could they be so heartless? Was the younger brother safe? These thoughts kept him occupied, and kept his craft headed toward shore. By evening he had washed up on the beach by his village.

He went stealthily to his wife's sleeping place. She was overjoyed to see him, for the hunters had returned and told that he had drowned. Though the youngest brother insisted that he had seen him still alive on the rock, the villagers had chosen to believe the older men. They knew of the rivalry between the other hunters and Natsilane, but that was to be expected. They regarded the boy's version as wishful thinking, for they knew how fond he was of Natsilane, but the young wife had kept hope in her heart.

"Natsilane, you are here!" she exclaimed. "I was afraid I would never see you again."

"Hush, my dear. Do not wake the others." He held her to him. "I am here for just a short time. Tell nobody that I came, not even your brothers."

"They leave again in a few days for West Devil Rock."

"Will your youngest brother go too?"

"Yes, he is going to try to spear his first sea lion."

He asked her to bring his carving tools to him. She did so and he said, "Remember now, not a word to anyone." Then he was gone as suddenly as he had come, leaving her to wonder. Was that really Natsilane? Or was it just his spirit? She had been drowsy from sleep. Had she just dreamed that he came? No, he had taken the tools.

Natsilane went into the woods, built a camp

and set about carving. He wanted to devise some way to avenge the treachery of his brothers-in-law. Remembering the Sea-Lion Chief's promise, he asked him for help. Soon he was deep into his work, inspired with an idea and carving with more ease and sureness than ever before.

But what was he making? It was a blackfish the likes of which had not been seen before, a killer whale, being shaped from spruce. First he shaped a large head, its jaw slightly open to show two rows of menacing teeth. Next he worked back on the body, scooping out the blowhole and raising the dorsal fin. Then he tapered the body down to the tail.

When he had finished carving the fish, he made a series of four pools on the beach, the fourth reaching out to the sea. He put the spruce killer whale into the first pool. It floated briefly, then sank to the bottom. He carved a second blackfish, this time of red cedar. When he placed it in the first pool, it floated awhile, jumped into the second pool, floated awhile longer, and then it too went to the bottom.

A third carving, in hemlock, made it to the third pool before sinking. He had been carving for several days, and his skill increased with each finished work. Inspiration was surging through him as he began to carve the fourth blackfish, this time from yellow cedar. When it was finished, Natsilane sang the songs of his ancestors and also a song to the sea lions. Then he launched the fourth blackfish into the first pool. It circled once, twice, and leaped into the second pool, where it again circled several times. It leaped into the third pool, circled rapidly, leaped into the fourth pool and swam out to sea. Natsilane was pleased with his creation.

"Thank you, oh thank you, Chief of the Sea Lions!" he said. Then he called the blackfish to him and gave it a command. "Go, mighty blackfish, go to my vengeful brothers-in-law as they return on the sea from their hunting. Destroy them and their boat. But spare the youngest boy, for he pleaded with them to save me."

The blackfish set out as he was ordered. It was late afternoon when he met the boatload of hunters, now only a short distance from their village. They were peering intently ahead, trying to make their way through the low fog that hung over the water. Blackfish came up to the boat from behind, unnoticed, and went under it. Rising suddenly, he capsized the boat and broke it in two. The boy was able to grab onto half the canoe, but the blackfish came between the others and the shore, forcing them farther out to sea.

The boy floated for a time almost in a daze. As he drifted atop the canoe half, he seemed to see people in the foggy distance. They were reaching out to those in the water, pulling them toward them. Had a rescue party come? Yes, yes! These were relatives of the hunters. Soon two of the brothers were coming toward him.

He was so glad to see them, so glad to know they were alive. Now they could go ashore together.

"Here, grab hold of the canoe," he called to them.

"We don't need that," the brother answered. "Come on. We're going where it's warmer."

The idea appealed to him. He was numb with cold and so tired of gripping the canoe. He had no feeling in his hands. The relatives beckoned to him to go with them. But what was keeping them afloat? He couldn't see any canoes. And they were luring him farther and farther away from the shore. Then he realized that these relatives were no longer alive. They had died recently, drowned while fishing.

Just then one came closer and held out a paddle for him to grasp. The paddle looked like a mink.

Then he saw that his would-be helper was a land otter and his canoe was a skate.

Was he delirious? Having hallucinations? Or were these the Land-Otter People his parents and grandparents had often told him about? Land otters came for drowning victims or people lost in the woods, and took them to live with them. But those who went with them never returned to the village.

Dazed as he was, he knew he wanted no part of them. His ancestors had also said that a strong will could resist the call of the land otters. He knew he must fight to stay alive if he wanted to return to his family in the village. He wanted to see Natsilane alive again and to become a great hunter like him. These very thoughts seemed to give him new energy. He kicked as hard as he could, pushing himself and the canoe in the direction of the shore. As the distance grew between him and his brothers and dead relatives, they seemed to fade into the fog. Then they were gone altogether.

He lost track of time as he slipped in and out of consciousness, but he clung to the canoe with a frozen grip. At last he felt land under him. He unlocked his icy hands from the canoe part and struggled up above the waterline before he fell down on the beach, unconscious. That was where the villagers found him and took him to his father.

The boy told the chief of the accident and of the strange blackfish that had upset the canoe. He repeated the story of the treachery of his brothers to Natsilane. This time they took him more seriously. Could the blackfish have been sent to punish them? The chief grieved for sons and heirs, and for Natsilane, such a fine hunter of sea lions and worthy husband of his daughter. Natsilane's wife wept for him and for her brothers. She had not seen her husband since the night she had given him his tools. She told her father about his visit. Why did he want his tools, they wondered. Could he have carved this new blackfish, the killer whale? Did he have the spirit powers to give it life? Was he a shaman?

Not long afterward a strange blackfish was seen near the beach, and at the same time a newly killed seal appeared on shore near the place where it had been. Was this blackfish the Killer Whale? At other times a halibut or sea lion would be found there. They did not know, of course, that Natsilane had instructed the blackfish never again to harm human beings, but to be their benefactor. As he continued to provide for them, the chief and the villagers realized that Blackfish, or Killer Whale, was a gift to them from Natsilane, who had gained supernatural powers. They took the Killer Whale for their crest.

The youngest brother became a great hunter and succeeded his father as chief of the village. He thought often of Natsilane, who became a legend in the village. There were those who claimed to have caught a glimpse of him riding the seas between two killer whales, holding on to them through the holes in their dorsal fins. But this is not known for certain.

FOG WOMAN

Fog Woman, an Earth-Mother figure, appears to have evolved from Volcano (Frog) Woman. In her role as food provider she is the prototype of the Greek Demeter, the Roman Ceres and the Egyptian Isis. In fact, she plays the traditional role of woman in human societies from the most primitive to the modern.

The Fog Woman story is an allegory with several messages: Like the medieval morality plays, it illustrates the consequences of pride, arrogance, selfishness and cruelty. Raven's inability to regain his wife and retain the wealth she had brought him, even though he has supernatural powers, demonstrates the finality of words spoken and acts committed. In the return of the salmon to the streams each year to provide food for the people, the story shows the virtue of forgiveness and the exercise of justice. The innocent are not deprived in the punishment of the transgressor.

In some versions of her story, Fog Woman produces salmon by washing her hair in a basket and pouring the water into the stream, and then withdraws the salmon by brushing her hair. This mystique-of-hair motif is as old as Medusa, Samson, Rapunzel and Stephen Foster's Jeannie, and as current as the fright wig and the Mohawk.

As the benefactress who brought the precious gift of salmon to the people of the North Pacific, and as the wife of Raven, Fog Woman is analogous to Persephone in the mythology of ancient Greece.

Persephone, daughter of Zeus by Demeter,

F O G   W O M A N

goddess of agriculture, was captured by Hades and taken to rule with him in the Underworld. In a compromise with her mother, however, Hades allowed Persephone to return to earth each year to promote the growth of food crops.

Fog Woman simply appeared, full-grown and beautiful. Raven, supreme being in Tlingit-Haida mythology, captured her by irresistible charm, and she left him of her own will, as mysteriously as she had come.

But each year Fog Woman calls the salmon back from the open ocean to the streams of their birth. They follow her call in such abundance that the people can take all they need for food, and still there are salmon to produce new generations.

Fog Woman was for a time the wife of Raven,
that ambivalent character who is the closest of any to a
deity in Tlingit and Haida mythology. Raven gained the
sun and the moon for mankind and transformed the
world and its creatures into their present state.

Raven first met Fog Woman when he was
lost in a fog. He was fishing in open waters with his two
slaves, Gitsanuk and Gitsaqeq. Since there were no
salmon in those days, the fishermen had left their
camp on the creek to try for cod or halibut or sculpin.
The weather was clear enough when they started out,
but while they were fishing, a thick fog suddenly
settled around them. Soon they could see no farther
than the end of the canoe, and no matter which
direction they paddled they could not find a way out of
the fog.

After they had been lost for several hours, a
beautiful young woman appeared as if from nowhere.
Even the world-traveled Raven was amazed. She was a
tall, slender woman with long, flowing hair and calm,
gray eyes. She sat in the canoe with an air of dignity, as
one used to giving commands.

"Give me your hat," she said to Raven in a
quiet, firm voice. Still stunned, the usually quick-witted
Raven continued to stare.

"Your spruce-root hat. Give it to me," she
repeated. This time he took off his hat and handed it to

her. She took it from him and turned it over with the crown down. Gradually the fog poured into the hat and the sky became clear. Raven, who had accomplished many amazing feats himself, was dumbfounded.

"How did you do that?" he asked in his most ingratiating manner. For though he could be coarse or cruel when the occasion demanded, Raven knew how to charm. The woman did not give away her secret, but just smiled serenely at him. Delighted to be out of the fog, Raven did not press the point.

"This person bears getting acquainted with," he thought, and invited her to go ashore with him. She agreed.

Raven soon found himself in love with the woman and asked her to marry him. She agreed and they settled at the head of the creek. On the long winter nights Raven regaled her with stories of his adventures.

"There was a time when there were no creeks," he told his wife. She listened with interest to his adventure, not revealing in any way whether she had heard of it before.

Many years ago, when I was very young and journeying about the world, I stopped at the home of my brother-in-law Petrel. There was no water to drink then, only the salt water of the oceans, and I heard that he had an everlasting spring of fresh water. He let me have a drink from the small pool below the spring, but would not let me near the spring itself. He kept it covered all the time and slept beside it at night.

I told him about all kinds of things I had seen in my travels, hoping he'd get interested enough to go out and see for himself. He just stayed put. Maybe he suspected what I was up to. He did invite me to stay the night, though. I kept

telling him stories until he finally fell asleep.
Then I slipped out and found some dog
droppings, and put them in his bed. He rolled
around in the mess in his sleep, and it sure
was funny when he woke up. I think he
forgot I was there. He couldn't imagine where
the stuff had come from, and he muttered
and fumed.

During his courtship and early marriage,
Raven had shielded the delicate ears of his bride from
the sordid details of his adventures. But now that the
first flush of love had worn off, he took no pains to
spare her feelings. He went on with his story:

Then Petrel noticed the stink, and he
rushed out to the pool to wash off. As soon as
he left I got the cover off the spring and started
drinking the fresh water. By the time Petrel came
back, I had the spring almost dried up. Oh, was
he furious! He leaped at me and almost got me,
but I was too fast for him. I headed for the
smokehole. I would have made a clean getaway,
too, but I was swollen so much with all that water,
I got stuck.

Petrel is clumsy, you know. He can't fly
nearly as well as I can, so he couldn't get up to get
me, and he put pitchwood in the fire thinking he
could choke me with the smoke. It did make a
heavy black smoke and lots of soot, and I was
actually gasping for breath, but I managed to inch
my way out through the smokehole.

My feathers were white before — quite
elegant, really. All that smoke and soot turned
them black. But black is more masculine and I
really like it better. Actually quite becoming, don't
you think?

F O G   W O M A N

Fog Woman threw back her head and laughed as Raven pirouetted for her approval. "You are a handsome devil," she agreed, and Raven, satisfied, went on with his story:

> Petrel was even more furious but, full as I was, he couldn't begin to catch me. I circled and zigzagged just to tease him. But water kept spilling from my mouth. The bigger spurts, when they reached the earth, became the larger rivers, like the Nass, the Stikine and the Taku, and the small drops made the streams.

Fog Woman never tired of hearing this story, since her home was on the creeks. And in time the creeks would become even more special to her.

One day Raven went off on a fishing trip with his slave Gitsaqeq and left Gitsanuk at home with Fog Woman. While they were gone, Fog Woman ordered Gitsanuk to go out to the stream and fill the spruce-root hat with water. As he was handing her the hat full of water he noticed a shiny fish swimming in it.

"Where did that fish come from?" he asked. Fog Woman just smiled. "What kind of fish is it?"

Fog Woman thought awhile. "Salmon," she said. "It's a salmon." Gitsanuk looked at it with great curiosity, for he had never seen such a fish. This was the first salmon to come to Alaskan streams.

"Now we must cook this fish and eat it before Raven gets home," she said. "He is so greedy he would not let us have any of it."

They had both seen Raven eat prodigiously and heard him tell about times when he had eaten whole animals by himself. He was proud of his voracious appetite and he liked to boast of his skill in outwitting others. One time he persuaded some birds to kill a bear, and after it died he ate the whole thing.

21

He then caused the bear's wife to die by feeding her
halibut bladders filled with hot stones in place of fish,
and then he ate all of her meat, too. Another time he
killed a whale by flying inside it and lighting a fire.
When it died and washed onto the beach he devoured
it all. These revelations of cruelty and greediness made
even the self-possessed Fog Woman shudder. Lately
he had also shown a mean streak in dealing with her
on several occasions.

Fog Woman gave Gitsanuk detailed instructions for preparing the fish.

"First dig a pit in the sand and line it with
rocks. Then build a fire in the pit and place more rocks
on the hot embers. While the fire is burning, pick
skunk cabbage leaves to wrap around the fish. When
the rocks become hot, place the wrapped fish on them
and leave it there to bake."

Gitsanuk did exactly as told and brought her
the fish when it was baked. She ate some first and then
gave the rest to him. He had never tasted such a
delicacy. When he finished dinner, he put halibut on
the still-hot rocks for Raven's dinner.

"Be sure to put the salmon bones in the
stream," Fog Woman told him. "The remains must be
returned to the place of their birth to ensure plentiful
fish next season." He had barely done so when Raven
returned.

"Ah, I see we have halibut for dinner
tonight," he said, eyeing the fish on the warm
embers. "All of you are going to have to make do with
kelp and berries, though," he went on. "I've had a
hard day and I will need all that fish."

When he sat down to eat, the slaves set the
fish before him. But the sharp-eyed Raven spotted a
shred of red meat on Gitsanuk's teeth.

"What's that?" The slave became flustered
but did not answer.

"That red stuff in your mouth. What is it?"

The frightened Gitsanuk soon blurted out the whole story. Raven ate all of the halibut before calling his wife to him.

"What's this salmon that you and Gitsanuk have been eating?" he snarled. "Where did it come from?"

"The stream," she said matter-of-factly. "The slave scooped it up in the spruce-root hat."

"So the slave said," Raven mused. Then he remembered how she had caught the fog in the same spruce-root hat. "But how did it get in the stream?"

"That's my secret," she answered.

Raven knew enough not to try to get things from her by force, so he beamed one of his most winning smiles.

"And what do I have to do to be let in on this secret?" He was temporarily at her mercy if he wanted some of the fish.

"First you have to build a large smokehouse here on the riverbank," she told him. "I will go up to the head of the creek to wash my hair. After three days you should go out to look for salmon."

Raven wasn't one to follow other people's instructions, especially his wife's, but he wanted this new fish badly. He knew from the fog incident that she must have some kind of exceptional powers, so he did as she told him.

He spent the full three days building a huge smokehouse, for he was hoping for great amounts of salmon. He had to work alongside the two slaves, for although he had pressed them into service from the start, the job was too much for them to handle alone. Such hard work was unusual for the lazy Raven, who could generally trick someone else into doing his work for him.

On the fourth day he left the two slaves to

put the finishing touches on the smokehouse and went out to see whether he could see any fish yet. The bay at the mouth of the stream was choked with the silvery salmon. He looked up in amazement and saw his wife standing beside him.

"Let us walk up the stream," she said. But they could go only a short way, for the stream was choked with salmon.

"Look at all these fish!" Raven shouted. "Let's catch some for dinner."

"We can do that," she said. "Then we must catch many more to smoke and store for the winter." Raven was glad now he had built such a large smokehouse.

Fog Woman had Raven prepare a pit with rocks and build a fire in it while she filleted a fish and wrapped it in skunk cabbage leaves. She had a hard time keeping him from eating the salmon before it was ready, but when he tasted the luscious fish, he was in ecstasy. Though he had traveled throughout the world and eaten everything edible he came across, he had never tasted anything like this salmon.

After he had gorged himself on mounds of salmon, he settled back for a nap.

Then Fog Woman sent him and the two slaves out to catch more salmon. They brought them in by the boatload. There were the large kings with black spots and black mouths. Their meat was the most delicate. The smaller sockeyes with the finer speckling and red flesh were rich and delicious, too. There were the cohos with silver disks on their tails, also tasty. There were the humpback pinks, and chums with large dogteeth, not so tasty but nourishing. All these different kinds of salmon Fog Woman had brought to the streams.

While the men fished, Fog Woman cleaned and filleted each fish and then laid out the pieces on racks in the smokehouse. When the racks were filled, she had the men string lines and she hung the fillets over them to dry in the sun. While the fish were smoking and drying, she had the men build storage boxes. When the preserved fish was ready, it was stored in boxes and carried into the house. Soon the house could hold no more boxes, so Raven and the two slaves built a shed to store more. There would be enough fish for several winters.

"We are rich!" Raven shouted, and jumped around in excitement.

They feasted on salmon all summer and continued to dry and store more. Raven had never worked so hard in his life.

For a while Raven enjoyed the luxury of his riches. That winter he could stay comfortably at home instead of going out in rain and snow to look for food. But he was not really a homebody and soon he became very restless. He had never stayed with one woman so long, and his wife was beginning to bore him. Some days he would ignore her; others he would abuse her. One day in a fit of irritability he hit her with the backbone of a salmon that he had just cleaned of its meat. The sharp spines drew blood. Humiliated by his treatment of her, she ran from the house.

Then Raven realized what he had done. Fog Woman had filled the streams with the most delectable fish he had ever tasted. She had taught him how to prepare and store them, and his larders were still overflowing. Besides, she had been a warm and understanding wife and he really did love her. He ran out after her. When he got close enough to grab her, she slipped through his fingers. He tried several times to take hold of her but each time she slipped away. His fingers went through her like mist. Then she seemed to drift out over the water.

Raven was inconsolable. Would she return?

He remembered how she had first come to him from out of the fog. Who was this woman? Was she human or a spirit?

But the resilient Raven quickly bounced back to his wily self.

"At least I am rich. I will have no trouble finding myself a very desirable wife." While he was thus reassuring himself, he heard a strange swishing sound. Then he saw his dried salmon return to life and stream down to the water. Even the salmon that had been stored in boxes came to life and went out to sea, following the vanishing Fog Woman. The only reminders of his wealth were the salmon tracks on the beach leading to the water, and the smokehouse, the drying rack and the storage boxes he had built.

Raven, poor and again having to rely on his wits, set out in search of food and shelter. Not a salmon was to be found anywhere. Fog Woman had taken back her precious gift.

In the spring of the following year, fishermen wondered about the fingerlings that appeared in the stream, all moving toward the ocean. Then as summer approached, they saw great runs of adult salmon headed from the ocean to the mouth of the stream. Even when they had filled their canoes again and again with their catches, many salmon were left to go upstream to spawn. Eventually the fishermen realized that the spring fry were the result of the fall spawning, and that they would eventually return from the ocean as adult salmon, some to be caught for food and others to head upstream and reproduce.

Some say that the Creek Women who live at the heads of the streams are Fog Woman's daughters. These same people say that salmon return to spawn in the streams of their birth to catch one more glimpse of the Creek Women before they die.

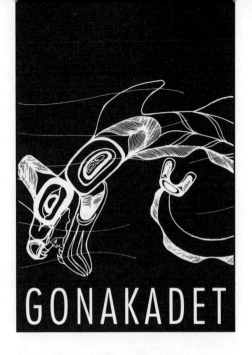

GONAKADET

The hero who became Gonakadet is akin to the Greek Prometheus, who was clever enough to trick Zeus and obtain the edible parts of sacrificial animals for human use. Zeus, like the Norse Wotan, planned to destroy man and replace him with a superior species, and so he withdrew fire from humanity. But Prometheus stole fire from Hephaestus and gave it back to the people. For punishment Zeus had Prometheus chained to a mountainside, where an eagle fed on his liver. But Prometheus was immortal, so his liver kept *regenerating, and eventually Hercules set him free.*

The young hero of the Tlingit-Haida myth also succeeded by his cleverness. When famine threatened to destroy his people, he tricked the lake monster, entered its skin, and through its power provided food in abundance. His antagonist was his abusive mother-in-law, who convinced the people as well as herself that she had supernatural powers and that she was responsible for their salvation.

Though the hero did bring about the downfall and death of the arrogant mother-in-law, vengeance was not his motive. He risked his life to benefit the people. By his temporal death he achieved immortality as Gonakadet, the lake monster, who still brings good fortune to those who see him.

GONAKADET

A young man of a fine family married a girl of the same status from a neighboring village. The couple decided to live with her parents in a large community house where her father was chief. From the start the young man got off on the wrong foot with his mother-in-law, a domineering woman, who was very jealous of her position as the chief's wife. She disapproved of the young man's gambling and lack of ambition. As the son-in-law of the chief, she felt, he should spend more time preparing to be a leader and successful hunter.

It was not unusual for the young men in those days to spend their free time playing the stick game. Each stick was carved as a different animal and had a certain value, with the devilfish as trump. The game was played in somewhat the same way as poker. The son-in-law, in his easygoing way, spent many hours playing with the other men. Too much time, his mother-in-law felt. He would return to the house late at night, often to a cold dinner, which he would have to eat in the dark. His mother-in-law would see to that.

"Let the fire go out," she ordered the servants one night after dinner. "We have finished eating." Then she turned to her daughter. "Why can't your husband come home in time for dinner?"

"He'll be here soon, Mother. He's probably working."

"Gambling, more likely," she grunted. "That

lazy fellow is a shame to us. You could have married any of the high-class young men of the village. We gave many blankets and carved boxes for your dowry."

"He's from a good family too, Mother, and will make us proud of him. He's just getting acquainted with the other men."

"Why doesn't he sit in the cold water with the other men and observe the preparation rites? I never see him with the men when they are coming back from their baths in the morning."

"Maybe he bathes in secret. Perhaps they did things differently in the village he came from. Oh, here he comes now." The young man came in and hugged his wife.

"Sorry I'm late."

"I guess you have been cutting down trees for firewood," his mother-in-law suggested.

"Tomorrow," he smiled. "Don't worry so much." His manner was always easy, but he was not so casual as he seemed. He had reasons for what he did.

"Why don't you take some responsibility around here? The chief's son-in-law should be building his strength for hunting and raids to bring our house honor and wealth."

"I'm working on it."

"By gambling?"

"You had better eat," his wife interrupted to change the subject. "The food is cold and the fire is out."

"That's all right. I'll get to bed soon." He ate his dinner and then lay down to rest. When he was sure everyone was asleep, he slipped out and went to sit in the icy water. He liked being alone when he bathed, for he was working on a plan to catch Gonakadet, the good-luck monster that the people talked about in this village. He had heard about this sea creature from conversations with the young men who

played the gambling games with him. The story
appealed to him and he made it a point to play as often
as possible, to learn more about the mysterious
monster. He put together the various details and
started to work out a plan for catching the monster.

To build his strength and become worthy to
receive spirit power, he spent much longer sessions in
the water than the others did. During the long bathing
periods he worked out an idea for a foolproof trap. But
he was secretive about everything to keep the others
from wondering what he was up to. He could not have
people getting excited and following him. Any
commotion would scare the creature away.

Summer came and it was time to camp closer
to the fishing grounds. They found a spot not far from
the village. As the days wore on, the fishermen brought
in their boatloads of salmon and put the fish out to dry
for storage and winter use. Not far from the camp was
the lake where the monster was believed to live. When
the fish runs became more scarce toward the end of
the season, the son-in-law packed some dried salmon
and got ready to go to the lake.

"Where are you going?" his mother-in-law
asked. "Now that the salmon are harder to catch, you
take off. We don't have enough fish yet to last the
winter." She didn't mention that his catch had been
larger than anyone else's in the village.

"While our salmon is drying I'll check out
some other streams," he said. "Maybe the runs will be
better when I get back." Then he went to find his wife.

"I am going to the lake," he said softly to her.
"I have built a cabin and will stay there for a while."

"Are you going to watch for the monster?"
she whispered.

"Yes."

"Have you seen it?"

"No, but I know it is there. I'll get it."

"How will you do that?"

"I have a plan. But we mustn't tell anyone. People would make too much noise and scare it off. I need to surprise it."

"Then I won't see you for a long time."

"No, and I'll really miss you. But when I come back I should have something that will make you and all the families of the house proud of me." He kissed her goodbye and set out for the lake.

As he got near the lake, he could hear the loons' plaintive warble and the crows' sharp replies. Yellow skunk cabbage was in bloom along the path and wild lupine and pink fireweed colored the green patches of the meadow. Ravens were teasing an eaglet in a nest high in the trees. He put his things in the cabin and then set to work on his trap. First he cut a tall cedar so it fell across the water and the ends were supported by the banks on each side of the lake. He split the tree lengthwise from the top nearly to the roots and tied the ends together with more roots. He wanted to make sure they could hold under great strain. Then he made crosspieces, which he inserted in the middle section of the split tree to hold the two sides apart at that place. Using some of the dried salmon as bait, he let a line down between the crosspieces. Then he waited.

It was some time before he noticed any action, but finally the line moved. He pulled it up quickly, but in his excitement he jerked it too suddenly and broke the line. He spliced the line, baited and set it again, and then waited for an even longer time. To pass the time while he had to sit very still, he tried to visualize the sea creature from the things his gambling cronies had said. It was supposed to look something like a whale, a large one. But it had ears and claws and a tail, all of which looked as if they were made of copper. It was probably very strong, too.

Suddenly the line moved. The young man moved quickly, but this time pulled steadily and evenly on the line. The monster was heavy and pulled against him. It took all his strength to get its head up into the trap. By degrees he pulled the head up through the slit in the log and held it there while he kicked out the crosspieces, letting the two sides close on the head. The monster fought even harder now, pulling the tree under water in the struggle.

After more than an hour it died and the trap surfaced, still clamping the monster's head. Again it took superhuman strength to open the trap and pull the monster to the edge of the lake. Once he got it ashore, he sat down exhausted. While he rested he looked at his strange catch. There were ears and claws and a tail as the men had said, all with a coppery sheen. When he began skinning it, he noticed the sharp, strong teeth they had mentioned. This was the legendary sea creature, all right.

After the skin had dried for several days, he tried it on and slipped into the water. He would be the monster. Suddenly it began to swim and headed down toward the bottom of the lake. It took him to a beautiful house with carved posts and carved and painted boxes. It was the monster's home, and just like the more luxurious longhouses in the village. But it was finer than any of the others he had seen.

When they came back up, he took off the skin and hung it to dry. The next morning he hid the skin in the hollow of a tree and went back to camp. He told his wife how he had built the trap and struggled to get the monster into it. He also described the monster and told about putting on the skin and visiting the monster's home.

"I have hidden the skin in the hollow of a tree. When I wear it, I think it will bring me good fortune in hunting things from the sea."

His wife's face lit up. "I knew you would bring honor to our family and our house."

"We still can't tell anybody about it. We must wait to see what the monster will do," he told her.

The salmon lasted through the winter, but, as the mother-in-law had predicted, it ran out before the next fishing season. Famine threatened.

"There is little to eat in the village. Can't your husband lead a fishing party to try to catch something?" the mother said to her daughter.

"I'll ask him," the wife answered and went to find her husband.

"I'll look for food," he said, "but it will have to be after dark." She knew without asking that he would wear the monster skin, and she was frightened. It might take him to unknown places and not let him return.

"Be careful, my love," she whispered.

"Look for me at dawn before the raven calls. If I do not return before its call, do not look for me any more." She wept softly as he bid her goodbye.

He made his way back to the lake and found the skin in the tree where he had left it in the fall. He took it out and spread it on the ground by the shore. Such a strange creature. Gonakadet, the men had called it in their stories. It was supposed to bring good luck to those who caught sight of it at sea. Maybe it would bring him luck as a fisherman and hunter. He got into the skin and floated out onto the lake. Then he dived and went down toward the monster's house, and on beyond it to a stream that led to the sea. He moved with such speed that it did not take him long to catch a salmon, leave it on the beach in front of his mother-in-law's house and return to the lake. He put the skin back in the tree and was home before the raven called. His wife was relieved and happy to see him.

The next morning the mother-in-law was out

early, even before the young men had gone out to bathe. As she poked around for clams or mussels, she came upon the salmon.

"What's this?" She tried to pick it up, but it was too heavy. "What a huge salmon! How firm its flesh is. It must have just come in on the tide."

She called for help from the house, and soon there were several to help carry the salmon.

"This should be enough to feed the whole village tonight," said the chief, who had come down to the beach with his daughter.

"Where did it come from?" she asked her father.

"Your mother found it on the beach. She has asked me to go and invite all the village people to dinner."

The husband came in when the fish had been cleaned and set by the fire, ready to be baked. "What a fine fish," he said.

"No thanks to you," retorted his mother-in-law. "Maybe you could cut some wood for the fire, if that's not asking too much. We will need lots to make hot coals for baking it."

Guests and hosts alike were in good spirits as they feasted on the fresh salmon, the first since last fall. It had been days since they had eaten even dried salmon. The mother-in-law enjoyed being honored as the one who provided the food.

The next night the young man set out to try his luck with the skin again. This time he brought in two salmon before dawn. He was sound asleep in the house before his mother-in-law found them. Again she had her servants prepare the fish and invited all the people in the village to share it.

The following day she was up at dawn to see whether the fish would continue to come in. This time there were four salmon.

"Your luck is holding," the young man said with a wry smile.

"It's a good thing," she rose to the bait. "You have certainly done nothing to help the chief provide for this house. With my luck we have been able to feed the whole village."

When they were alone, the young man said to his wife, "Tonight I will try to bring a halibut. A large one should last a few days."

"My mother has told my father to order everyone to stay away from the beach in the mornings, because she had a bad dream, she said. I think she doesn't want anybody else to find the fish that's left."

"That's good. I want her to be the one to find it." He enjoyed being able to fool her in this way. True, the "luckier" she became, the more sarcastic she was to him. But he would have the last laugh. "Look for me before the raven calls."

The mother-in-law's "luck" continued. The halibut was found the next morning. The next week there was a seal.

"I wonder what is bringing me this luck," she said to her husband that evening. "It must be my spirit powers."

"You have brought fortune to the village. The seal meat should last at least a week. Without the food you have given, the whole village would starve. The people made many speeches in your honor tonight."

"This good fortune will make us wealthy and highly respected. I must thank my spirit helpers." The young man laughed at her boasting. She even blamed him for the famine when she spoke to the women around her.

"It's our son-in-law's laziness and gambling that caused our lack of fish," she told them. "The sea creatures were unhappy that he did not bathe or follow the preparation rites."

"Maybe he brings his strange ways from his former village," the women tried to sympathize. "But you have saved us." The young man overheard these things but did not try to defend himself.

The next day she told her husband to have a spirit mask made in honor of the Food-finding Spirit. "I will need a headdress too, made of bear claws."

He hired the finest carver to make these things. He also ordered an apron for her, trimmed with puffin beaks, and some rattles of shells and rings. These were things a shaman would wear.

When the mask and headdress and clothing were finished, she put them on. She really thought she had received a shaman's spirit powers.

After dinner with the village people that night, she decided to put her outfit on for them. As she modeled it, she swayed slightly to the movements of the dance, shaking the rattles lightly for a beat. The apron swayed with her, causing the puffin beaks to clatter in rhythm with the shells and rings of the rattles. Soon she was dancing more intensely. The headdress sat heavily on her head and nodded to the people in rhythm with her movements. The crowd became hypnotized, for she looked like a shaman. Her dancing became wilder. Then she stopped suddenly and looked out over the crowd.

"My spirits are speaking," she sang out. All became quiet. After a long wait, she went on. "Tomorrow I shall find two seals on the beach."

In her excitement she probably did not know how much she really believed she was a shaman and how much she was pretending.

If she were thinking more clearly, she would have realized that she had not made any of the necessary preparations — bathing, fasting and other rites. She had gradually let herself believe that she had special powers, not giving any thought to the terrible consequences of being a false shaman. She was sure her "luck" would continue.

When she discovered the two seals the next morning, her taunts were greater than ever. "Leave some scraps for the sleeping man," she told the people who were cutting and preparing the meat. They laughed and joined in the ridicule. The daughter was embarrassed, but the son-in-law said nothing.

"Why does she make those nasty remarks?" the wife asked her husband.

"Maybe she has a feeling I might be connected with getting the fish and seals, and she is afraid the people will find out."

"Now she is demanding a sea lion. They are dangerous."

"I'll be careful. I should be back before dawn."

When the mother-in-law found the sea lion, she was ecstatic, certain now she had found favor with some spirit. She ordered the people not to gather wood on the beach front, but to go behind the houses for wood.

"We must leave room for the Food-finding Spirit to bring fish ashore." Then she started ushering guests into the house. "Come to the feast. We are lucky to be able to eat of the tasty sea lion. It has been this way from olden times. The chiefs of our house have always been lucky."

"She is behaving as though she had spirit powers," scoffed the young man, "and the people are being taken in by it."

"What started as a game for you has turned into a contest between the two of you," said his wife. "You must stop now. She has asked for a whale."

A whale would be terribly difficult, he knew, but how could he stop now? He could not let her get the better of him.

A few days later he landed a whale on the beach, but not without a great struggle that lasted until just before dawn. His wife had been frantic with worry. But he got home just before the raven's call. He must not tempt fate again. Exhausted, he slept the whole next day.

"This morning Mother found the whale you left," his wife said when he finally got up at nightfall. "The villagers have been singing her praises all day. After the feast she put up many boxes of oil. The villagers are buying it and the whale meat she had packaged. They look on her as a great lord."

"That won't be good for her when her luck runs out. They'll know then that she deceived them."

"She continues to taunt you."

"Her jeers don't bother me. I know my luck comes from the skin I wear. But if I should die when I am out, set my body inside the skin in the place I usually hide it."

"Don't speak of dying." His wife shuddered. "The spirits will protect you," she added, probably to convince herself. "But do not try to bring in another whale."

"I'll stay with fish and seals for a while." He too had been shaken by the close call, and he kept his promise for a time. But again the challenge tempted him.

About two weeks later when dawn came, he had not yet returned. At the raven's call his wife looked out at the beach, but he was not there. She ran down to the water's edge, where she found her mother examining two whales.

"Have you seen my husband?" the daughter asked. But the mother was wrapped up in her own excitement.

"Look at the two whales my spirits have sent," she said. "But what's that between them? It looks like a beast." The girl stared at the whalelike creature. It had two long ears, two fins on its back, and a tail. It was the monster her husband had described to her.

"Oh, my husband!" she cried. "Now you are here on the beach, dead. Why did you have to die like this?" Then she turned to her mother. "Where are your spirits now, you fraud? You say you have spirits, but you don't. That is why my husband lies dead on the beach."

"Your husband? Where is your husband?"

"Is this your Food-finding Spirit? How is it that your spirit should die?"

"Are you mad, girl? This is a sea monster," her mother answered. Then the girl called to the villagers who had come onto the beach.

"Some of you who are very clean, come help me. Look in the monster's jaw and you can see my husband." Two men stepped forward and held open the jaws while two others pulled the husband out.

"The raven must have called as he tried to get out," said one of the men.

"Your husband was our benefactor?" her mother gasped. "The man I called lazy? It can't be." She looked dazed. "Then I have no spirits." She paced back and forth, her eyes glazed and frantic. "Your husband, wearing the monster's skin, brought the fish, the seals, the whales. Oh my shame! My shame! Where can I hide?"

She ran toward the house. But before she got halfway, she began to go into convulsions. The women ran to her as she fell to the ground. In a short time she was dead, with blood gushing from her mouth. She had been shamed before the village and had died of her shame.

The grief-stricken girl ordered the men to take her husband's body in the skin up to the lake.

"You will find a large tree there with a hollow. Set them inside."

When the men had carried out her orders, they saw the cedar tree lying across the lake. "Look! This is the trap he used to snare the monster. It took a lot of planning to come up with something so tricky. That young man was clever," said the leader of the group.

"He had to be strong, too, to bring that creature in," said another. "He must have sat in the icy water and chewed devil's club in secret."

"He had spirit powers, the spirit of Gonakadet," said the leader. "He is the one who provided the food for the village. The woman was a fraud."

"She has been punished. It is dangerous to make false claims to spirit powers."

For weeks after her husband's death the young woman was overcome with grief. She went often to the lake to weep by the hollow tree. She wept for her misguided mother and her dishonored father. But mostly she wept for the husband she loved and would never see again.

One evening when she was at the lake, her husband appeared to her. But he looked strange. "This must be my husband's spirit," she thought. She watched him get into the skin that had been placed in the tree. He became Gonakadet. He motioned to her to come to him and she went. He took her on his back and the two went down to the beautiful house beneath the lake, so rich in carved pillars and painted boxes. Its walls were hung with furs and blankets. They made it their home.

The chief grieved again, this time for his lost daughter. But the story that the young man had become the luck-bearing Gonakadet won new honor for the chief. Sometimes villagers would catch a glimpse of Gonakadet swimming in the sea with his wife. Success in everything they undertook came to all who saw them. Good luck would also come to those who saw their children, the Daughters of the Creek, who live at the heads of the streams.

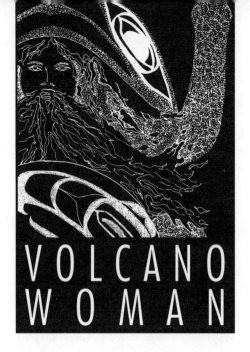

VOLCANO WOMAN

*Volcano (Frog) Woman, sometimes
known as Dzelahrans, may be the oldest
and most revered of Tlingit-Haida myth-
ological figures. She is believed to have
reached Alaska from Asia, with late
migrants who came by sea. Her coun-
terparts figure in some Asian mythology,
as well as Egyptian, Babylonian, Greek,
Phoenician, Roman and Norse. She is the
Earth Mother, and as Volcano Woman
she is historian, collective memory and
guardian of tribal tradition. She destroys
an entire village for the failure of its
people to observe the proper rituals and*

show respect for living creatures and cherished objects. Only a young girl, who had observed the puberty rites, and her mother, who tried to divert the people from their sacrilege, are allowed to live and find refuge.

Volcano Woman's harsh judgment upon the villagers is provoked by two instances of sacrilege: the cruel behavior of the village's young prince and his cohorts toward Frog, and the prince's mistreatment of the Cormorant Hat. This hat was held in highest esteem. Made from the skin of the spectacled cormorant, the hat was no doubt intended merely to protect the wearer from rain, but it accrued symbolic value as it was handed down from generation to generation.

Frog, a figure of consequence out of proportion to its size, is highly respected and even feared. He still appears as a clan crest.

V O L C A N O   W O M A N

One warm, sunny day during the salmon season, a young prince called his three companions to him. "Let's paddle over to the creek and spear some salmon," he said to them. The prince's whim was their command, but this was an order they really warmed to.

"Let's take things to camp out for a few days," cried one. These boys were a little older than the prince, and as his constant companions they were expected to look after him. Since they were all still too young to take a man's place in the fishing boats, they generally had to be satisfied with fishing the streams.

It didn't take long for them to stock the canoe with their spears and provisions and carry it down to the water. When they were getting into the canoe, the prince decided to go back to the house for his father's Cormorant Hat. As he was headed out with it, his father stopped him.

"You had better not wear that hat," he said. "You are not ready for it yet."

"Why not? Soon I'll be old enough to wear it at our feasts."

"Much responsibility goes with wearing the Cormorant Hat. Your grandmother would advise against it too, I'm sure."

"The Cormorant Hat is greatly revered by the clan," his grandmother said. "You are not mature enough yet to treat it with proper respect. If you are not

careful, something might go wrong. Something bad
could happen." But the boy insisted and his father let
him take the hat.

"Be very careful with it," he called out as the
boy ran down to the beach.

As soon as the prince returned to the canoe,
the boys set off in high spirits. The canoe moved easily
across the water and it was not long before they
reached the mouth of the stream. They carried the
canoe ashore and set it high above the tide line. Once
they had a fire crackling and the camp set up, they
began to fish with their spears.

The fish were not so plentiful as they
expected, and the prince began to get irritable. His
Cormorant Hat, still a little too big for him, kept falling
into the water. He finally picked it up and beat the
water with it.

"You stupid hat! What use are you? You just
keep getting in my way." Then he tossed it onto the
beach of the stream. He had forgotten his father's
warning.

By sundown the boys had caught a few fish
and set about preparing one for their dinner. They
filleted a large, firm fish and cut it into pieces to be
wrapped in skunk cabbage leaves and put on the hot
coals to roast. The prince spread out a large leaf and
reached for a piece of salmon. Seemingly out of
nowhere, a frog jumped onto his clean leaf.

"Get out of here, you pest!" he scowled and,
picking up the frog by a hind leg, flung it into the
bushes. He spread out another leaf and reached
for the salmon again. Again the frog leaped onto the
leaf.

"Git!" he cried, flinging the frog into the
bushes. A third time he got a fresh leaf and put the
salmon on it. This time the frog jumped onto the

salmon.

"That does it!" he cried and threw the frog into the fire.

"Why did you do that?" the youngest companion asked, dismayed. "Now we're all in for it." He repeated the warnings the prince's father and grandmother had given him about treating animals with respect.

"That's right," said a subdued prince. "My father also told me to be careful with the Cormorant Hat," and he began looking around for it on the bank. When he found it, he brushed it off carefully and set it in the canoe. The boys' high spirits dampened a little. But one of the older companions tried to cheer them up.

"Oh, don't believe everything those old women say," he said to dismiss their fears. "They have been telling those tales for years."

"Look at him skittering around in there," said another older boy, pointing to the frog in the fire. He grabbed his spear and pinned down the struggling frog.

"Listen to him crackle!" Soon the boys were laughing and joking again, forgetting all apprehensions. They got fresh leaves to wrap their fish and put it on the coals to roast. While they waited for it to cook, they cleaned and washed the rest of the salmon and stored them in the boat. After they had finished eating they retired for the night, forgetting the incident of the frog entirely.

During the night they heard the voice of a woman wailing, "Oh, my child! Give me back my child!" They got up and looked all around the camp, but they could find no one. But once they settled down to sleep, they could hear the woman crying for her child again.

The next morning they decided to try their luck farther upstream. The fish were really plentiful there and they landed quite a few. But all the while they were fishing, they could hear the woman calling for her child. "Oh, give me back my child! What have you done with my child?"

When they had caught all the salmon they could carry, they got ready to go back to the village. During the whole time they were cutting and cleaning the fish, the voice continued.

"Give me back my child, my only child, or your village will be destroyed." With some alarm, the boys started for home.

"What do you think that is?" asked the prince. "It makes me shiver!" The older boys were not so quick with their answers this time.

"I don't know," said the oldest. "Maybe it does have something to do with the frog." And they began to paddle faster. All during the trip home, they could hear the voice of the woman crying, "Oh, my child! Oh, my child! What has happened to my child?" It was as if the woman were hovering over their canoe. The prince did not know what they could do to satisfy her. They could only go back to the village as quickly as possible to warn the people.

As soon as he got to the village, the prince hurried to tell his father about the woman's crying and her predictions. But he failed to mention the frog and the Cormorant Hat. Although his father listened with interest, he did not know what to make of such a strange story. He put it to the wild imaginings of young boys and humored them.

"It sounds as if you had an exciting time," he said. "Take your fish to the women now. Your mothers will be pleased with your catch."

But before long the people in the village could hear the woman wailing, "Oh, my child! Oh, my child! Give me back my child or your village will be destroyed." They thought the predictions were

strange, but didn't know what to do about them. They
went on with their chores in the usual way. One of the
old women, however, was concerned. She suspected
that the boys had been up to some kind of mischief and
went to see the chief.

"I think the boys have done some thoughtless thing that is more serious than they realize," she
told him. "You should pay more attention to these
warnings and have the people make preparations to
escape while they can. Something terrible may be
about to happen."

The men with the chief laughed at her. "Oh,
you worry too much, old woman," the chief answered.
"If we had to leave the village every time some boys got
into mischief, we would be moving all the time."

"If you want to survive, get ready to move,"
the woman pleaded. The chief was now becoming a
little concerned, but he did not want to risk the scorn of
his men.

"Get along now," he said more harshly. "We
are getting ready for a feast and we have work to do."

Then the woman went through the village,
warning others of coming danger, but no one took her
seriously. So she began to make her own preparations.
She dug a large underground chamber at the rear of
the house and equipped it with enough food and water
to last several months. There she installed her daughter, who had just reached maturity and needed to be
kept in seclusion. Then whenever she heard the
woman's wailing, she would run to the shelter and wait
with her daughter. Many of the people ridiculed her,
but some of the elderly ones grew concerned.

"We should try to find out what the cries of
the wailing woman mean," they said. "Perhaps our
young people have broken a taboo." But they could not
concern the rest of the tribe with their fears. The
people went on with their feasting and revelry.

One evening while they were making merry they heard distant rumblings. They paid no attention. As the night wore on, the rumblings grew louder. Soon they noticed smoke in the distance and they became alarmed. When smoke and fire broke out on the mountaintops, they started to run. But then came louder thunderclaps and the fire swept down the mountain in a torrent, destroying everything in its path. The people ran toward the water, but the volcano had already destroyed their canoes. They had nowhere to turn and soon were consumed in the fire. Only the old woman and her daughter, who had hidden in the underground chamber, were saved.

Many days passed before the noise and confusion settled. When the woman and girl were out of water, the old woman cautiously opened the door to the dugout. She could see and hear nothing. She started toward the village, but where was it? The entire village with all its inhabitants had been wiped out.

As she was returning to her dugout with water, she could hear the voice of the wailing woman: "I knew your uncles would avenge you, my son. The boys should have given your body back to me. But they destroyed it by fire, so your uncles have killed them by fire."

"What child has been killed?" the old woman wondered as she returned to her dugout.

Many days later the woman again came out of her hiding place to see whether others had perhaps escaped the fire of the volcano.

"Is anyone there?" she called as she went about. "Has anyone survived the anger of the supernatural being?" She received no answers. After many days of trudging about, the old woman became desolate. She went back to get her daughter and their few belongings, and together they set out to find a

village where people might have survived.

"Has anyone escaped?" she continued to call. No one had. Half dead, the two women came to a village that had been only partly destroyed. There were no people, but they found a canoe hidden in the brush. They loaded their things into it and put it into the water to paddle up the stream, hoping to find a good place to camp for the night. As they settled down to sleep, they heard the voice of the wailing woman.

"Your uncles have been avenged," she wailed. "The thoughtless ones have perished."

The next morning as they were paddling up the stream, the same one where the prince and his friends had fished, they saw a huge frog in the water. It looked like a human being and was wearing a layered hat. Its eyes seemed to shine like copper. As the frog swam away, they could hear the wailing woman sing, "Oh, my child! Oh, my child! Your uncles are at peace now that they have destroyed the proud ones."

Then the old woman and her daughter saw a woman standing at a distance on shore. She wore a labret in her lower lip and held in her hand a cane topped with the picture of a frog.

"This must be the revered Frog Woman," the mother thought, "and the 'child' that was killed was a frog." Then she knew for sure that the volcano had been sent as punishment for disrespect to the frog. Now Frog Woman would be known as Volcano Woman. She had spared the mother and daughter, but to what purpose?

After a while their provisions ran low and the two survivors were wandering aimlessly in search of food. Exhausted, they sat down and began to weep for their friends and relatives. All of a sudden Eagle swooped down before them.

"Why are you weeping?" he asked.

"We weep for the loss of our people. Our whole village has been destroyed," the mother said.

Then she told him the story of the volcano and the appearance of Frog Woman.

"You have been saved by Frog Woman, who is very dear to our clan," Eagle said. "I will take you to my people." Then he took each of them under a wing and flew to his village. When he had set them down, he changed to his human form and addressed the mother.

"We are now at the home of the Eagles. I am of this clan. We know that you are of high class, you have respected traditions and your daughter has recently completed the puberty rites. I would like to make her my wife."

The mother was greatly relieved that they were among friendly people who respected their status. Gladly she gave her daughter in marriage, and they lived comfortably in the Eagle village. All held Frog, or Volcano, Woman in highest reverence.

BLACKSKIN

Blackskin is the Hercules of Tlingit and Haida mythology.

Unlike Hercules, who strangled two serpents while he was still a babe in his crib, Blackskin appears to be a weakling, lazy and indifferent. He builds his strength in secret, and only after he is able to wrestle Strength to the ground does he reveal his great physical power.

Other Greek mortals had failed to kill the Nemean lion with sophisticated weapons, but Hercules, as one of the twelve labors he had to perform to become a god, killed the lion with a wooden club.

Blackskin's arrogant brothers, each confident that he could avenge an uncle's death, failed to kill the monster sea lion and lost their lives in the attempt. Blackskin tore the monster in two with his bare hands, a feat no less heroic than any performed by Hercules.

On another level, the stories of Blackskin and of Samson, the Judeo-Christian hero, are positive and negative presentations of the same moral. Blackskin, though born to be a loser, gains exceptional strength, honor and wealth by following tribal rites with exceptional diligence. Samson, born for heroism, violates tribal ethics when he consorts with the enemy, the Philistine Delilah. He is not only shorn of his prodigious strength along with his hair; he is blinded and enslaved. Though he regains his strength through fervent prayer, he destroys the enemy at the cost of his own life.

They called him Blackskin because his skin was sooty from sleeping too near the fireplace. His relatives, especially his two brothers, were ashamed of him because he slept late instead of taking the purification baths in the morning with the other young men. This was not fitting behavior for a nephew of the chief.

"How's the weakling this morning?" the older brother asked when he returned from bathing. "You're finally up."

"Talk about lazy — and dirty!" chimed in the other brother. "You could use a bath."

"Let the boy alone," said his uncle, the village chief. "Some day he will surprise all of us." He shook the boy's shoulder affectionately. "It's hard being the youngest." Once or twice when he was wakeful, the uncle had noticed the boy going down toward the water after all were asleep. Once he spied him coming in just before dawn.

"He's got his own plans," the uncle mused. "I like that." And he kept the boy's secret.

Then the terrible accident happened. The uncle was killed in a sea-lion hunt, hit by the flapping tail of the huge bull sea lion.

Since spears and bows and arrows were used for hunting at that time, the men could not shoot from a distance. Shooting from a moving boat, often on rough seas, was not usually successful either. They

55

had to get onto the big rocks with the animals. Often
the hunters surrounded a herd of sea lions to attack
several at once, before they were alerted to slip into the
water and out of reach.

It was in this kind of hunt that the uncle was
hit by the sea lion's tail. The other hunters carried the
body to the boat and brought it back for a funeral, with
honors and festivities befitting a chief.

Blackskin was desolate at his uncle's death.
He had admired the powerful hunter and wanted to be
like him. He felt that the uncle had liked him, too. He
went now to pay his last respects. He looked at the
dead chief, propped up in a sitting position to allow his
spirit to get out easily and travel to Spirit Town, where
it would stay until it returned to the family in the body
of a newborn baby.

"I wonder whose body my uncle's spirit will
inhabit next," Blackskin thought. Of course, the person
was not born yet. "I hope it will be someone worthy of
him." The chief looked so noble in death, dressed in
his finest robes and headdress. The body had been
prepared by the women of his wife's phratry. To hurry
his return to the living, the women had cut a lock of his
hair and put it in safekeeping with some other personal
belongings.

The eight-day mourning period had begun. A
wake of three or four days allowed friends and relatives
to come from a distance to view the body and pay their
respects. Blackskin listened to the songs of the women
mourners, who had cut their hair short. He watched
them dance, carrying large sprays of hemlock and
cedar. He saw the long, carved ancestral pipe passed
among the guests for the men to smoke. The men were
seated on the lower tiers around the fire. The women
sat on the upper tiers that lined the walls. Members of
the two phratries faced each other from opposite sides
of the house.

The smoke feast took place just before the body was cremated. Then the ashes were placed in a storage box and the larger remains were wrapped in a blanket. Later they would be put in a mortuary pole carved for that purpose. Then the feast began. Venison, bear meat, halibut, salmon, seaweed and other greens were among the many dishes also prepared by the women of the wife's phratry. Blackskin especially liked the berries and eulachon oil that were like dessert.

After the banquet, the ancestral stories were told. Blackskin never grew tired of hearing these tales of heroes who had brought honor to his clan. He hoped he too could bring honor to his people some day. At the festivities, deceased members of the clan were remembered. Then gifts were given to all the guests. Those who had prepared the funeral service and banquet received the most valuable things — copper shields, blankets, and food boxes and spruce-root baskets carved with intricate designs.

When the mourning period was over and the last guest had left, the young men began special rites in preparation for the sea-lion hunt. They vowed to find the bull sea lion that had killed the chief and tear it in half with their bare hands. But first they would need strenuous exercise and training. They got up at dawn to sit in the icy water, and then to whip one another with hemlock or spruce boughs to toughen their skins and make the blood circulate. They fasted and drank devil's club juice.

Blackskin did not join the men, for he knew they would only make fun of him. But he wanted to help avenge his uncle's death. When the others had fallen asleep after a big dinner, he would go out to sit in the water in secret. Sometimes he stayed so long he had barely enough strength to crawl up to the house. He would go close to the fire and lie in the ashes and soot. That is where the others would find him in the morning — black from head to toe. Only his aunt, the widow of the dead chief, knew his secret and encouraged him.

"Try to stay in the water a little longer each day," she urged. "Then you will build your endurance gradually." He kept up his nightly training.

In the mornings his two brothers competed for top position among the other young men in training. They had come up with a plan for testing the strength of the men and seeing whether they were ready to take on the bull sea lion. At one end of the village was an old tree with a young limb growing out of the base. After the men had bathed and switched one another with branches, they would run to the old tree at the end of the village. One by one they would try to pull the newer limb out of the base. Then they would run to the other end of the village, to a spruce about eight feet tall, and try to twist it at the roots. Day after day, the young men flexed their muscles at these tasks, but nobody succeeded in either of them.

Blackskin generally kept his distance from these activities, pretending to show no interest in them. But he kept on bathing in the cold water a little longer each night and switching himself a little more vigorously afterward. One night while he was bathing, a small man appeared suddenly on the beach.

"Where did he come from?" Blackskin wondered. "And what does he want at this hour of night?"

The small man seemed to read his thoughts. He came to the place where Blackskin was sitting.

"I am Strength," he said. "Let's see how strong you are. Come wrestle with me."

Blackskin was amazed. "Strength?"

"Strength of the North Wind," announced the little one.

Blackskin got out of the water and crouched

down to wrestle. The two circled. Then Strength pounced and after a short scuffle threw Blackskin to the ground.

"We'll have to wrestle again," he said. "You are not ready yet to test your strength against the village trees. I will come again after you have trained longer."

Blackskin slept in mornings and he rarely saw the other young men. On the occasions that he did see them later in the day, they would shove him and taunt him for his laziness. "Hey, Blackskin's getting tougher," the older brother said once after shouldering him but not budging him. "We had better watch out. He might be the one to overcome the trees!" His cronies laughed, but Blackskin just bided his time.

About two weeks later the small man showed up again to challenge Blackskin to a wrestling match. Again they crouched, circled and scuffled. This time Blackskin threw Strength to the ground.

"Now you are ready to try the trees," Strength said, and led him to the old tree with the new growth. Blackskin grabbed the newer limb and pulled it out on the first try.

"Put it back securely in the socket," Strength directed him. Blackskin cemented the limb in the socket with moistened dirt. Then they went to the young spruce at the other end of the village. With just as much ease he twisted the eight-foot tree to its roots. At the small man's command he straightened the tree again.

"Now you are ready to fight the bull sea lion," said Strength, "for you are stronger than the North Wind."

The next morning the older brothers trained as usual. The men seemed more feisty than ever as they switched one another after the ritual baths. They were impatient to get on with the hunt. After bathing they made their usual trek to the old dried tree. The older brother gave a hard jerk on the new limb and pulled it free. Cheers went up, and they all ran to the young spruce. There the younger brother grabbed hold of the trunk and twisted it to the roots. A second round of cheers went up.

"Now we are ready to fight the sea lions with our bare hands," the older brother said. "Our training period is over."

The long boats were fitted out with supplies and the strongest men were chosen to go. Although he was not among the chosen, Blackskin too got ready to go to Sea Lion Rock.

"Aunt, do you know where my uncle's weasel-skin hat is? I would like to wear it to the hunt." The older brothers had not given much thought to the tradition of wearing the ancestral hat with honor and receiving spirit powers. It had not occurred to either of them to wear the hat. The aunt was pleased with the boy's request.

"The weasel is the spirit helper of our family," she said as she gave him the hat. "Wear the hat with pride and treat it with respect."

"I will try to bring honor to you and the family in avenging the death of your husband, my uncle."

"Good luck, Nephew. You have trained well for the fight and you are strong. I hope you will fight well."

When Blackskin showed up on the beach, the men were surprised. Gone were the dirt and grime. The tall young man stood before them cleanly dressed and wearing the weasel hat of their uncle. But still they refused to let him board the boat.

"The men have been picked. Only the strongest can go," said the older brother, "those who trained all during these many months. You have slept in every morning." He ordered the men, now all in the boat, to push off from the shore. But Blackskin held the boat and kept it from moving, although all the men were paddling. The men pushed against his chest with their paddles.

"Go home and take care of Aunt while we are gone. You can help with the housework," taunted the younger brother.

At this Blackskin became angry and pulled the boat half out of the water onto the beach. In their hurry to be rid of him and get on their way, the men did not notice that he had pulled the canoe onto the beach with all of them in it. They thought the tide had washed it in again.

"You will need someone to bail the boat," Blackskin reasoned as they all got out of the canoe to lift it back into the water.

"You can come along to bail," said the older brother. "After all, you are a nephew, too." He had been noticing a change in Blackskin. He looked stronger and more self-assured.

The canoe load of hunters set out from the west coast of Prince of Wales Island, toward Sea Lion Rock in the open ocean. Large swells were rolling in and the waves were twelve to fourteen feet high. But the rowers were strong and the boat skimmed easily over the water. The high waves washing into the boat kept Blackskin busy bailing. As they approached the rock, they could see the water shooting twenty to thirty feet in the air as it hit the big rock.

In such rough water the approach to the rock was tricky. The men paddled intently to get the canoe close enough for the hunters to jump onto the rock, yet keep it from dashing against the rock and breaking. The oldest brother crouched in the bow of the boat. As the wave crested near the rock he jumped and landed on the very edge. When he got his balance, he moved swiftly toward the resting sea lions. He seized the smaller animals in his way and knocked their heads together to kill them. When he got to the big bull, he caught it by the tail and tried to tear it in half. But the crusty old beast raised his flipper and smashed the man against the rock, killing him, just as he had killed the uncle.

By this time the middle brother had jumped onto the rock and caught his balance. He reached the mighty bull, but the bull dashed him, too, against the rock and killed him. The hunters in the canoe were amazed and frightened. If the two brothers, who had apparently met the test of the trees, could not kill the bull seal lion, what could they do?

Then Blackskin strode toward the bow, breaking the thwarts with his shins as he came, wearing the uncle's weasel-skin hat and keeping his balance despite the rough water.

"I will avenge the death of my uncle, and now of my brothers," he said with authority such as they had never heard from him before.

He reached the bow, stood poised until the right moment, then leaped and landed upright on the rock. He picked up the smaller sea lions by their tails and dashed their heads against the rock. The medium-sized, he killed with a single blow to the head. Then he picked up the huge bull by the tail and tore it in half lengthwise. The hunters in the canoe were dumbfounded.

Then Blackskin picked up a dead sea lion and tossed it into the canoe, and then another, and another, until the canoe could hold no more. There was meat for all.

The news of Blackskin's feat spread rapidly through the village. The people were amazed and greatly relieved to learn that Blackskin was, after all, worthy of being the nephew of their dead chief. They paid him the honor and respect due a great man and made him their chief.

Blackskin never used his great strength to do ill, but only good. No longer did the people have to chop down trees when they needed wood for fuel. Blackskin simply broke off a tree, then dashed it against the rocks and broke it into fireplace lengths. When logs were needed for a new house, Blackskin broke off the trees, tore off the limbs, carried the logs out of the forest and hoisted them into place. In many other ways, too, he provided well for his people, and as he had hoped when he was a boy, he brought great honor to the tribe.

BEAR MOTHER

Bear Mother, Rhipsunt in some versions, is an Earth-Mother figure associated with the peoples who occupied Southeast Alaska before the latest Asian migrants came by sea.

Although Bear Mother came by her role as punishment for ignoring tribal taboos, she achieved heroic stature as the vessel through which the bloodlines of her people were strengthened and new knowledge and skills were introduced.

The Bear twins, who spent their early years with their powerful Bear kin and then, in human form, enhanced the power and status of their mother's people, are reminiscent of Romulus and Remus in a small way. Those twin sons of Mars were reared by a wolf and later made use of the survival skills thus acquired in the early stages of founding Rome.

By his sacrificial death to release his sons to human life, the Bear Prince, like the Pacific salmon which spawn and die so their progeny can thrive, suggests the essential purpose of all life.

One sunny day in August, a princess and
three companions set out to pick salmonberries. It was
the salmon season and the people were living at the
summer camp, where they had been busy for weeks
cleaning and drying sockeye salmon. The weather was
warm but not hot, and the air was fresh after the rain of
the day before — a perfect time for berry-picking.

The princess and her companions paddled
across the bay in a canoe, to a hillside where many
kinds of berries were growing. The morning sun had
dried the rocks and logs along the beach, but drops of
water still clung to the bushes and tall grass.
Chipmunks chattered in the trees and gulls walked on
the beach looking for food in the outgoing tide. The
girls could see berry bushes higher up the hill. After
working their way through the brush, they came upon
the tall salmonberry bushes.

"Here are some nice, ripe ones," called one
of the girls as she approached a bush of yellow berries.

"There's one with big, dark red berries up
the hill a little farther," said another girl.

"But you have to climb through prickly
bushes to get to it," said the princess. "We don't want
to get our legs and arms scratched."

So they picked at the lower bushes. The time
went quickly and soon it was late afternoon.

"My basket is overflowing," said one of the

girls. "How are you doing?"

"Mine's full too, and so is the princess's," another answered. "The sun will be going down soon. We had better get back to the canoe."

They started through the woods, singing to warn the bears of their presence. But soon the princess began chatting. "I think my parents have been talking to suitors. I heard that the relatives of a very handsome Bear prince have visited."

"We saw some of them last week, but I think your parents refused them," the first girl told her.

"Why do they always refuse my suitors?" the princess asked peevishly. "I wish I could choose one."

"We should not be talking here," said the oldest girl. "We should be singing to warn the bears."

"You really believe that, don't you?" said the princess, but she stopped talking for a while and joined in the singing. It was true that she was her parents' darling, the only daughter among many sons. Her brothers idolized her, too. They were all great hunters and brought many furs for her robes.

"Did you see my new marten robe?" asked the princess, who had grown tired of singing. "My grandmother has finished sewing the skins and it is lovely." She continued to chatter on similar subjects as she followed her companions through the woods. Suddenly her feet went out from under her and she was on the ground. She had slipped on bear droppings.

"Darn those stupid, dirty bears!" she yelled. "Why don't they watch where they do their messes!"

The girls were shocked and somewhat frightened at her outburst. They did not want the bears to blame them for these insults. But they helped her clean up and they all started down the path again, singing their songs. Then the strap on the princess's basket broke and her berries scattered on the ground. Again the girls hurried to help her.

"I can get the rest now," she told them after they had picked up most of the berries. "Go ahead. I'll catch up." They were only too glad to get going.

In a few minutes the princess was on her way and had almost caught up with the girls when her strap broke again. She quickly picked up the berries she could find and ran to catch up with the others. She knew she should hurry, for the sun had gone down and it was getting hard to see in the woods. But she was having trouble carrying the basket with its broken strap and watching her footing too. As she was struggling along, a good-looking young man appeared on the path beside her — out of nowhere, it seemed.

"Where did you come from?" the startled princess asked.

"I have been sent to help you," he said, taking the basket from her.

"How nice of my parents to send you. They must have been worried about me."

Her parents had always been very protective of her. She was beautiful, just growing into womanhood, and had many suitors asking to marry her, but her parents discouraged all of them. Now, when this handsome guide appeared in her path, she thought he might be the prince her parents intended her to marry, the suitor whose relatives had visited recently. While they were walking, it grew very dark and the princess had no idea where they were.

"It's getting so dark. Why don't we stop at my home?" her guide suggested. Trusting him as someone sent by her parents, the princess agreed, and he led her into something that looked like an opening in the hillside. But once they were inside it, it was like a large room. She saw people wearing bearskins seated around a fire.

"This is my family," he told her. "Hello, Father. I have brought home a bride."

The princess was surprised at first, and then very happy. Her parents had chosen this handsome man for her husband! It was the custom for a young girl of marriageable age to be kept in seclusion while suitors came to ask for her hand. The relatives of a young man interested in marrying her would take his request to her mother and clansmen. The mother or uncle of the suitor would say, "I value the words I am about to speak at forty blankets" — or thirty, or fifty — the gifts he would bring if his proposal were accepted.

"Perhaps two days from now I will speak to you," the mother would answer. Then the relatives would leave and return later with the forty blankets. If the parents accepted the visitors' kinsman for their daughter's husband, they would be given the blankets, which they then would distribute to their people. In return the father would give the parents of the bridegroom blankets, carved boxes and other decorative items as a dowry to show that he respected and valued his daughter. Often the girl did not see her husband until her wedding day.

"Maybe they have made all the arrangements already," she thought. "But it is strange that they did not say goodbye." Things were happening too quickly for her to give the matter much more thought.

The chief rose and welcomed his son and his bride. He called together the people and presented his son's bride to them. Then he gave a feast in honor of the young couple.

The princess lived happily with her husband's people for a while. It wasn't long, however, before she started to notice strange things. The most unusual was the way the fire would blaze up when the fishermen shook their wet rain gear over it. As the drops fell on the fire, they would light up in a mysterious way. Since her husband fished all day and came home only long enough to eat and sleep, she did not have a chance to talk to him about these things. She thought maybe if she went out on the next fishing trip, she could get to know him better and could learn more about his people. At first he refused her request. "You are a chief's daughter and are not used to such hard work," he said.

"But I want to be with you. I've watched the women at home and even helped sometimes." She continued to plead and he finally gave in. It would be nice to have her there.

At the camp while the men fished, the women gathered wood for the fires. As she had always done at home, she gathered the driest wood she could find. But she noticed that the other wives were picking up water-soaked wood.

"I wonder how they will light a fire with such wood," she thought. But she did not say anything. When she had enough wood, she stacked it in a pile and then made her fire the way she had seen her people do. It was burning brightly when her husband came in from fishing. He took off his wet coat and, like the other men, shook it into the fire. Instead of blazing up brightly, the fire went out. She couldn't imagine what had gone wrong and was embarrassed when he had to dry himself and cook their fish at someone else's fire. She noticed the other women with their hands to their mouths, hiding their smiles, and was afraid that she had humiliated or annoyed her husband. If she had, he did not let on. He was proud of his beautiful wife and loved her.

They returned home as the sun was getting ready to set and went right to bed after their hard day's work. The girl tossed and was unable to sleep, thinking of all that had happened that day. Finally she dropped off, but slept fitfully. She woke suddenly in the middle of the night, feeling something furry next to her, and sat bolt upright.

"What's this animal doing in my bed?" she gasped. It was a huge grizzly bear.

Wakened somewhat by her outbreak, the bear sighed and turned toward her. But now he was the man she knew as her husband. She nudged him.

"I must have been dreaming," she said to him. "What an awful nightmare. I dreamed that a bear was sleeping beside me." As she was speaking, the real situation began to dawn on her. Her husband was a Bear! She had been captured by the Bears! Her grandmother had told her that animals could take human form when they wished. Some of the mysterious things that had been happening began to add up.

"You are a Bear! I have married into the Bear tribe!"

"Yes, we are Bears," her husband admitted. "I had asked your parents many times to let me have you for my wife, but their answer was always no. The only way to get you was to take you by trickery. My father agreed to let me capture you because he wanted to punish you for the disrespectful things you said about the Bears."

She remembered her angry outburst after slipping on the bear droppings. Her companions were right to have scolded her. Maybe if she had sung the songs to warn the bears, they would have spared her.

"Now I know why my fire went out, and why the drops glistened when shaken into the fires made with wet wood. I have heard that this happened with the Bears' fires.

"I want to go home," she cried. "I miss my mother and father and friends."

"This is your home now," her husband tried to soothe her. "You have lived here for three years now and have two lovely children." He pulled her close to him and stroked her hair. "I really do love you."

Her husband's attentions won her over for

the time. When she was with him, he held a certain power over her. But when he was away from her, she felt the strong longing for home again.

All the time the princess had been missing, her family was wondering what had happened to her. When she had not returned to the canoe with her companions, her parents and brothers were much upset. Since it was dark by that time, they waited until the next morning to start a search for her. They traced the path the girls had taken to the berry patches, but there was no sign of her anywhere. Then they noticed the berries she had dropped on the path when she fell. There were bear tracks on each side of her footprints. They remembered the story the girls had told the night before, about her slipping on the bear droppings and becoming angry with the bears.

"The princess must have been killed by the Bears," one of the searchers said sadly. But the people continued to look for the body, since they knew that the Bears did not eat human flesh. After many days the chief went to the seer.

"She is not dead," the seer said. "She will be returned to us one day, but you must continue to search for her. She is not far away." Her father and brothers kept looking for her every time they went out hunting. When the salmon season was over, they returned to their winter home.

It was spring again and the Bears were getting ready to go out to the summer camps for the fishing season. At her old village the people, too, were getting ready to move to the camp not far from the place where the princess had been lost. Since it was early spring and animals were coming out of their winter places, her brothers decided to go hunting before going out to fish. They went in a direction they had not taken since their sister's disappearance. It was in the direction of the Bears' home.

"There should be plenty of game in this area," one of her brothers said. "It has not been hunted in a long time." At the same time, the family members were still determined to find the princess. First the chief sent out the oldest brother.

"You are my oldest son and the finest hunter in the village," the chief said. "It is here that my daughter was lost, maybe even captured. If so, you are the one most capable of finding and recapturing her."

The oldest brother set out with a handpicked group of hunters, but after three days returned without the girl. Then the second brother took along another group of able hunters to help him, but he did not succeed either. The father finally chose his own best hunters to go with the third brother, but their attempts were also futile.

Each time the brothers set out, the princess's husband knew about it through his special spirit powers and knew what the outcome would be. Each time he hid in his home in the mountain cove and was safe. The third brother had come quite close to finding him, however.

When the third brother's attempt failed, the chief was deeply grieved.

"Now my daughter is lost forever," he wailed.

All the family members were grieved with him. But the princess had a younger brother who had not yet gained much experience hunting and was never allowed to hunt alone. Only on special occasions had he been allowed to go out with older hunters to learn from them. Since she often played with him and their dog, Maesk, while the older brothers were out hunting, he was the princess's favorite brother.

"I'll go find my sister," the youngest brother volunteered. The older brothers all laughed.

"How will you do that when the best of

hunters haven't been able to find her?" asked the

oldest. "You have never been out alone and don't know these mountains. We will have to look for you, too, if you get lost."

"Maesk will lead me to her, won't you, girl?" he said, petting her fondly. He continued to plead with the chief. Finally the chief agreed to let him try.

When the youngest brother set out with Maesk and a group of hunters, the Bear husband became very sad. His spirit powers told him that the dog and the youngest brother would find him and kill him. Quickly he spread devil's club around the cave to hide the scent of the princess from the dog.

When the young brother and the hunters reached the foot of the hill where the Bears' cave was, Maesk barked in the direction of the cave. The young man scanned the mountain, looking for an opening or some movement. The shrubs were all varying shades of green, from the new spring yellow-green of the alders and willow to the blue-green of spruce and hemlock. There were only a few traces of snow left. But the young man could see no signs of the princess, and devil's club disguised the scent so the dog could not pick up the trail. She darted here and there, trying to pick up the scent, stopping periodically to bark. The princess must have heard the barking, for at this time she looked through an opening. She saw the dog surrounded by the hunters.

"My dog Maesk has found me!" she said with joy. Her husband was in the back of the cave making his preparations for death. He did not hear or see her, nor was she aware of what he was doing. She was overjoyed at the thought of seeing her family again. She scraped some snow from the ledge and pressed it into a snowball. Then she threw it down toward her brother. The brother saw the ball rolling toward him and picked it up. As he turned it in his hand, he noticed fingerprints on it.

"Here, Maesk. Here, girl, smell this," he said, holding the snowball to Maesk's nose. The dog began to bark again, furiously. This time as the brother looked up, he saw something moving high up on the bare hillside.

"I think somebody's up there. That must be where the snowball came from," he said. "Let's go!" The trail was almost impassable, but the group struggled up it. Maesk and the youngest brother were the first to reach the ledge at the entrance to the cave.

The husband came out of the cave. "Wait awhile, my brother-in-law," he called. "My spirits tell me that I must die, but first let me sing the dirge that I will pass on to my children. With it I will give them my spirit powers."

The young brother hesitated, not knowing what to do. But soon his sister was at her husband's side. "Do as he says, Brother. He wants to make our children great hunters before we return to our people." The brother did as she asked.

When her husband had finished singing his dirge, he called his children, who were now in the form of bear cubs, to him. He turned them into human beings and said, "Go now with your mother's people. You will become the greatest of hunters." Then he turned to the young brother. "Shoot me now with your arrow," he pleaded. But the young man was reluctant.

"Come! Be quick!" The young man drew his arrow, and the other hunters arrived just in time to see him shoot the Bear husband. The princess wept for her husband and sang his dirge over him. Then she left his body to be tended by his people. She and the children returned to her village with her brother. The children grew up as human beings and became the greatest hunters their people had ever had. Their tribe became renowned among all other tribes as the one with the greatest hunting skills.

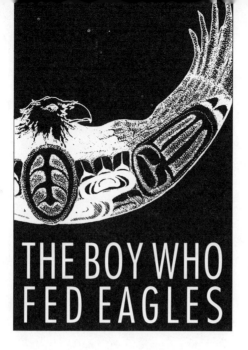

THE BOY WHO FED EAGLES

The situation of the Boy Who Fed Eagles is similar to that of Telemachus, son of King Odysseus of Ithaca in Homer's Odyssey. *Telemachus is too young to assume the authority of his absent father but he observes the laws of the gods in the face of derision and threats from older men of status.*

The Boy Who Fed Eagles, though slow to mature physically, is scrupulous in paying homage to the Eagle, his clan crest. He suffers the scorn of his scoffing kinsmen, and is left behind when famine threatens and the villagers must go in search of food.

Athena rewards the dutiful Telemachus by reuniting him with his father and helping them overcome those who threatened them. Telemachus inherits the kingship upon his father's death.

The boy's reward comes from the eagles he had fed. They bring him food in such abundance that he grows rich and powerful, and succeeds his humbled uncle as chief.

THE BOY WHO FED EAGLES

The boy sat under the spruce tree, out of the rain and out of the sight of the men loading the canoes. It was only a light, steady rain today, not the kind that blew up under your cape, and it was definitely warmer than it had been. Spring and the fishing season were here. The boy's hat and cape would have kept off the rain well enough, but he did not want to face his cousins.

"Aren't you coming along?" his older cousin had asked the night before.

"Not this time. I'll just fish the streams," he had answered.

"It's time you quit playing around the creek and come out fishing with the men," his cousin replied. "You're old enough to do a man's work now." A man's work meant going out to sea in a twenty- to thirty-foot canoe, fishing until it was loaded and, after unloading it at the village, going back out if it was early enough. The fishing day was the twelve to fifteen hours of day-light at that time of year.

"He would rather catch the tired fish coming back to the streams and feed them to the birds," another cousin scoffed. "He's not strong enough for a man's work."

The boy did not answer. There was no point to it. They always ended up making fun of how thin he was. Like his cousins, he sat in the icy water and exercised every day, but he did not grow much.

The fishing canoes were lined up on the beach. Each was carved from a single cedar log and their bows were painted with house emblems. He could see Beaver, Salmon, Halibut, but no Eagle. The Eagle was the crest animal of his mother's clan. Like his cousins, he was being trained by his uncle to be the clan leader some day. It was the usual thing for a boy to be trained by his mother's brother. But he was really lucky to be trained by this uncle, the richest and most honored chief in the village. His uncle's words on his last birthday came back to him.

"You are a young man now. Continue to chew the devil's club and bathe and exercise. Honor the Eagle, our clan crest, and act in a way to become worthy of spirit powers. You must know how to fish and hunt well and must gain the respect of the people to become a leader."

The young boy had done as his uncle had said, but he was not yet ready to go out in canoes to fish. He had to feed the eagles that came to the spit, the long bar of sand and rock that hooked out into the sea and formed one side of the bay in front of the village. The eagles usually gathered at the far end of the bay around noon, and that is when he took the fish out to them. One of his older aunts encouraged this.

"The Eagle is our crest animal," she said. "People do not honor eagles anymore the way they should. In the old days we always left a part of the catch for them. But your cousins just laugh at me when I say this. 'Let them catch their own fish,' they say.

"Look at the eagles out there. They fly so high and are so strong," she went on.

"They glide so easily through the air," the young man added. "How proud they look."

"You must be like the Eagle," she said. "You must seek the Eagle spirit. Pay homage to the Eagle."

THE BOY WHO FED EAGLES

She did not have to convince him. He was already intrigued by the eagles' grace in the air and dignity on land. Once they had settled, that is. They were always a little clumsy in landing. They would thump to the ground and teeter, opening their wings to balance themselves. This made their feathers fluff out and gave them a rumpled look. But once they gained control, they sat very tall and still.

He was thinking of these things while he fished the stream. Now he had quite a catch, and it was about time to feed the eagles. He took a small canoe down to the water, put the fish into it, then rowed toward the far end of the spit. As he paddled, he looked down into the water and could see sea anemones opening and closing and jellyfish floating. He pulled the canoe up onto the beach, crunching the deep blue mussel shells and white clamshells as he walked. Birds or small animals had probably left them there after eating the meat. Chipmunks chattered in the trees nearby and a faraway loon called. Ravens were rummaging around on the beach for food. The boy sat to wait for the eagles.

In a little while he saw one circling its way toward the ground. Soon it was joined by another flying in the same descending spiral. One after another they dropped to the ground, staggered a little, and then found rocks to perch on. They sat tall and stared straight ahead. The boy stayed very still and kept his distance from the big birds. The nearest bird turned toward him and seemed to glare at him. The boy stared back. The piercing eyes seemed to be looking right through him. Did the eagle know that he was the one who had been feeding him? The boy kept looking into the eyes, almost hypnotized. Did the eagle know he belonged to the Eagle clan?

"Give me your Eagle spirit," he found himself saying. The huge bird continued to stare. The boy began to move very slowly and gently scatter the salmon on the beach. The eagles did not move until the boy was in the canoe again and on his way home.

The humpback run continued and the chief ordered the villagers to go out to sea each day to fish. All went except the boy. While the others were bringing in boatloads of fish from the sea to the women to clean and cure, the chief's nephew continued to fish lackadaisically in the streams. He would load his catch in a canoe and take it out to the spit for the eagles. As far as the women knew, the young man did not catch fish at all.

"There's no use trying to explain to them," he thought. "They think all the salmon should be cured and stored."

One evening the chief spoke to his nephew. "Why do you refuse to go out fishing with the men? Can't you see that this is embarrassing me?"

"I'm sorry, Uncle. I don't want to cause trouble. But I have to feed the eagles."

"You can feed them again after the humpback run is over. They can find food for themselves for a while. You have been listening to the women's stories. Let the women feed the eagles." The chief had a pretty good idea of who had been talking to the boy. He would have to speak to her.

The boy continued in his dreamy way to spear salmon and take it to the eagles that circled the spit.

He loved to sit on the point and watch the eagles soar and glide and then suddenly dip to land. Sometimes an older bird would rest on a branch out over the water. Mischievous ravens would squawk and dive at him, but he would just look out over the water as if they weren't there. Then they would go off to tease an eaglet in a nest high up in the tree, while the mother or father on a branch nearby gave them stern looks.

Like them, he did not let the village chatter about his laziness bother him.

As the summer wore on, the eagles grew fatter and began to drop their feathers. He saved the brighter, fuller ones to wear in his hair, hoping they would bring him Eagle power. Noble bearing and sharp vision are fine qualities for a leader.

Winter came and food was scarce. The young man was often hungry, for the chief had told the heads of the households to refuse him food. "Go to the eagles for food," they said, or, "You should have been storing salmon last summer instead of feeding it to eagles." Only his oldest aunt would slip him something to eat at night when nobody else was around.

"You paid homage to the eagles," she said. "Maybe we are short of food because the rest have not properly honored the eagle."

By March there was no dried fish left.

"We are going to have to leave earlier than usual for the eulachon runs this year," the chief announced. "The runs are still light, but maybe we can catch enough to last us until fishing season."

Eulachon were caught mainly for their oil, which was used like butter and cheese. It was used in cooking and preserving and was also traded for blankets or other needs.

The people got things ready to move. They also took rakelike tools and dipping nets for catching the fish, and large baskets to put them in. To get the oil from the fish, they would put hot rocks in the baskets.

"My nephew who has not fished with us is not to know that we are leaving," the chief told the people. "And you canoe leaders, none of you is to allow him into your canoe. The old woman who has been feeding him can stay here with him."

When they were ready to leave, he ordered the fires to be put out and all the food taken along.

But the old woman managed to hide a coal ember in a clamshell and to save out a little dried fish.

The young man continued to go out to the spit to visit the eagles and to look for clams and mussels. There were no salmon in the stream now. He gathered wood from the beach or the woods behind the houses for fire, which they were able to start with the coal ember from the clamshell. One night he was tossing and turning, having gone to bed hungrier than usual. He woke suddenly from a fitful sleep to what sounded like the screech of an eagle. He got up, slipped out of the house and headed for the point.

The sky was gray in the early dawn and there was a light rain. Soon things will begin to grow, he thought. Already he had been able to kill some small animals he found when he was out early in the morning looking for food. As he got nearer the point, he could make out something on the beach. He picked his way over the slippery rocks and found a salmon.

"How did this get here?" he wondered. "I guess it drifted in." He lost no time taking it up to the house.

"It hasn't been on the beach long," said the woman. "It is so fresh and firm." She cleaned and boned it and set it on the coals to cook. They ate well that day and had enough left over for several more meals. He put the head, bones and fins out for the eagles.

The next morning he again woke to the eagle's call. When he went out to the spit he found another salmon, this time with an eagle's claw mark on it.

"Look at the eagle sign on this fish," he said to the woman. "The eagles must be helping us." The woman examined it.

"That's very strange. Let us sing the Eagle song while we clean it," she said. The song was one she had learned from her grandmother and had taught the boy.

In the days that followed, many different gifts from the sea appeared, always announced by the eagle's call. The young man was sure now that the eagles were helping them. He was able to carry the salmon and smaller halibut and seals up to the house. But for the bigger fish and the sea lion and whale, he had to rig a pulley. He stripped cedar bark from the trees and coiled it into rope. Then he looped it around the branch of a tree over toward the house and caught one end around the large animal or fish. As the tide turned, the fish would float toward the house and onto the beach.

The young man and the old woman spent long days cleaning, boning and curing fish and getting oil from the seals and whale. They filled storage boxes and baskets and put them in their own house. Then they began filling the other houses with boxes and baskets until all were filled.

It was now two months since the people had left for the eulachon runs, and their catch had not been good. The chief spoke to them one evening.

"Our food supply is low. If we do not find more food we will soon starve."

"I wonder whether the boy and the old woman are still alive at the village," said the oldest nephew. "Maybe they have found some food."

"It's too early for salmon yet," the chief replied, "but I could send some servants to see what things are like there. We can't stay here."

As the servants approached the village, the young man recognized his uncle's canoes. He went out to welcome the visitors and invite them ashore. He was kind to them and offered them a fine dinner of many kinds of seafood.

"Where did you get all the different fish and

seal and whale meat?" the man in charge asked after dinner.

"We have been lucky," was all he told them. Then he showed them the boxes and baskets of food they had preserved. The next morning before they set out for the camp at the river mouth, he fed them well.

"Eat well, but do not take any food back with you. And don't breathe a word to anyone about the food you have seen here."

They all gave their word to keep mum and took their leave. One of the women, however, hid a piece of seal meat to take to her small child, who she was afraid was going to starve to death. When they got back to the chief's camp, she waited until dark to sneak the baby the meat. But it caught in the baby's throat and the baby began to choke.

"What is the baby's trouble?" asked the chief's wife.

"It's just coughing. It has a cold." The woman was afraid to tell the truth.

"Bring it here right away! It's choking." The chief's wife quickly put her finger down the child's throat and pulled out the meat. Now that it could breathe, the frightened child wailed. The chief's wife looked at what she had pulled out.

"This is dried meat. Where did you get it? We have not had dried fish or meat for some time." She thought perhaps the servants had hidden some food and were using it for their own families. Such treachery could be punished by death, especially when the people were threatened with starvation. The servants had to tell of the young man's good fortune.

"He served us a wonderful meal of salmon, seal, halibut and whale. Your nephew whom we left behind has plenty to eat," said the servant in charge of the journey.

"There is no room for all the meat and fat,"

said another servant, "or for the dried salmon, halibut, seal, sea lion and whale. Four large whales lie on the shore."

"How could he have caught so much seafood so early in the season?" the chief asked. "Surely he must have some spirit powers."

"Let us go back to our winter home," said his wife.

"And beg of a mere boy?" shouted the chief.

"But we will starve without food," his wife answered. The chief groaned. He looked at the hungry and sad faces of the people.

"It is what I will have to do," he said finally. "We will have to humble ourselves. We will have to agree to whatever he says."

"Yes, it will be hard, especially for you, the chief. But we will starve here without food," she answered.

The chief ordered the people to pack their belongings and load the boats. Then he called his two youngest daughters to him.

"Put on your finest clothes and jewelry and paint your faces to look your best. Your cousin will want to choose a wife now that he is wealthy. Since ours is the most honored house, he will want to choose one of my daughters, and you are the prettiest."

Since the girls were Ravens like their mother, it was proper for the young man, who was an Eagle, to marry one of them. The girls knew also that with his wealth and newly won honor, he would probably become chief of the village. They set about making themselves as attractive as possible. What better luck could they have than to be a chief's wife?

It did not take long for the canoe loads of people to be on their way home. As they came into the bay in front of their village, they saw fish scraps and grease floating on the water. Starving as the people

were, they scooped these scraps up from the water to
satisfy their hunger. The chief and his family kept their
dignity for a while. The two young ladies remembered
their manners for as long as they could. But when they
saw the others eating, they could wait no longer. They
too scooped up grease and scraps of fish and wolfed
them down. Only the oldest daughter, who was not so
pretty and did not wear such fancy clothes, controlled
herself. She sat quietly in the boat, waiting until the
young man offered them food.

When he saw the boats approaching, the
young man went out to meet them. In spite of their
cruelty to him, he was glad to see his relatives again.

"Welcome home, my people," he said to
them. Then he went to the chief's boat. "Welcome
home, Uncle."

"Thank you, Nephew. We are glad to be
home and to see you again. We are happy that you
have had good fortune and beg your forgiveness for
deserting you."

"You are forgiven. I do not hold a grudge.
The eagles have been good to me and I have received
the Eagle spirit. I want to use it for the good of the
village," he answered.

"All the houses are filled with storage boxes
and baskets of food," he told them. The people
cheered. "You are welcome to the food, but you must
pay for it."

"We shall give all of our wealth in exchange
for the food in our houses," the chief replied.

"Bring the canoes ashore, then, and get
ready to have dinner."

After they had eaten a fine dinner of all kinds
of food from the sea, the young man gave each guest a
package of food. To each of his uncles he gave half a
whale. The next morning the relatives came bearing
gifts in exchange for the food in their houses —

canoes, sea-otter skins, abalone shells and marten skins. The young man became very wealthy and was made chief of the village.

"Now it is time for you to choose a bride," the old chief said to his nephew. "You probably noticed my two pretty daughters."

"Oh yes, I have, and they are very pretty." He looked at the two girls dressed in their best. Their dancing black eyes had pleased him as a boy. But now he was chief. He looked at the older daughter with the noble bearing. She was the one who had not scooped food from the bay. "I think I would like this daughter to be my wife." The crowd oohed in surprise, but the uncle recovered quickly. He was happy that one of his daughters would be the new chief's wife.

"I also give a special place of honor in my house to the aunt who saved my life and helped me cure and preserve all the food," the new chief said.

As long as he lived, the eagles continued to provide him with salmon, halibut, seals, sea lions and whales, and he became wealthier with each year. And always he made sure the Eagle was given the honor due it. He remained chief until he died.

THE GIRL AND THE
WOODWORM

A relatively recent and localized story believed to have originated on Prince of Wales Island, "The Girl and the Woodworm" may allegorize the dispersal of an extended family — a splintering that occurred when the group outgrew its food resources, or conflict arose, or perhaps the departing group was attracted to some other location.

As a monster that must be slain for the collective good, the Woodworm is kin to assorted dragons, giants and other dreadful creatures — Goliath, Grendel, Fafner,

91

even the beanstalk giant of the English folktale — that appear in folk literature worldwide.

Only by some supernatural power could a mere woodworm become a monster menace, so no David or Beowulf, Siegfried or St. George goes forth alone to confront it. The men of the village share responsibility for the slaying, and thus share in the risk of whatever vengeance may be visited upon the killer.

The girl's mysterious power to raise the woodworm, her devotion and her death, make her a heroic figure worthy of memorializing in the new clan crest.

THE GIRL AND THE WOODWORM

A long time ago, the daughter of a powerful and wealthy chief was kept in seclusion at her coming of age, as was the custom in those days. She had to stay by herself in a corner of the family longhouse, behind a heraldic screen painted with her family and clan crests. Her place of seclusion was dark, for she was not to look at the sky. Nor could she look at any of the men, lest she bring bad luck to hunters, fishermen or gamblers. The only people she could see were her mother, her aunt and the servant who attended her. At this time she was also to observe many customs in preparation for her marriage, which was to take place soon afterward.

During the first eight days of her confinement, the girl was allowed only small amounts of food. For the first two days she had nothing to eat or drink. Her throat was dry and her stomach ached with hunger. At the end of the second day, her mother came to her with some water.

"Here, Dear, take a drink," she said, offering the water. The thirsty girl reached out eagerly, but her mother poured the water out onto the floor.

"Don't be greedy, Dear. You must take things slowly and graciously."

"But I'm so thristy, Mother, and my mouth is so dry!" she cried. "Last night I dreamed I was drinking from a large, fresh stream, but when I looked more closely I saw it was the dirty stream that runs under the house."

"I'll bring another drink in a while," her mother said, giving her an encouraging hug. The girl lay on her bed to wait.

When the mother returned about an hour later, the girl remembered her manners and took the water as slowly as possible. She tried to sip it, but the best she could do was to keep from gulping it down.

"It's so lonely here, Mother," she complained. "I hear my friends running and playing outside, and I miss being with them."

"Soon it will be easier," her mother consoled her. "Tomorrow you may have something to eat. After that you may have water every day and food every other day until the eight fasting days are over."

"I don't really feel hungry anymore. My stomach just hurts. But the worst thing is not being able to see or talk to my friends."

"I know. I had to go through the same thing. All young girls have to at maturity. But just think! Afterward you will be ready to marry. These few months will pass quickly after you get more used to them."

But the young girl was not so easily consoled. During the day she could hear children not much younger than she playing "mother and daughter" and pretending to "shut in" the smaller child. If they only knew! she thought. It was so much worse than they could imagine. It was hard for her to believe that just a few days ago she was outside playing with them.

Then one afternoon she could hear everyone getting ready to go berry-picking. Parents were calling to children to get their baskets and hurry down to the boats. She loved picking berries more than anything else, and they were all going without her. She wondered whether any of her friends missed her. Then came the quiet after they had all left, and she lay down on her bed and sobbed.

She made it through the eight days of fasting, but her loneliness grew. She could hear the rain on the roof and the trees blowing in the wind. She wished she could be running and skipping in the rain with the wind blowing in her hair.

One day when the slaves were splitting firewood, they found a woodworm in a piece of rotting wood. They left it in the paper-thin sheets of the log and slipped it into her room, intending to startle her. They hoped by teasing her a little they could cheer her up. But the lonely girl, instead of being frightened, took the worm for a pet.

"Well, at least she will have something for company," one of the slaves said.

The girl kept the woodworm hidden from her mother and her attendant. She tried to feed it a little oil, but it would not eat. Then she offered it other food, but it would not take that either. Finally she tried nursing it, and the worm drank hungrily. As time passed it grew steadily. She would cradle it in her arms and rock it and even sing it lullabies.

She didn't even have her dolls to play with now. She had had to "potlatch" them away to younger girls at the feast that was held in the village (without her, of course) when she was given her first food after confinement. She was not even allowed to weave baskets, because the dried roots and grasses might make her hands rough.

"Sit right here. Sit right here," she would sing to her pet. "See, it has a face already. Sit right here." Her mother and the attendant thought she was play-acting.

In the meantime the worm continued to grow and she had trouble keeping it hidden. It no longer nursed, but got its food by raiding the boxes under the floor where the dried fish and grease were kept. After some time it had tunneled its way underground from house to house until it had eaten most of the winter supplies of the village.

"Some monster has been stealing our provisions!" the villagers said in alarm, but no one was ever able to find it.

One day while the girl was singing, her mother peeked behind the screen. There sat her daughter rocking the huge worm.

"It has a mouth already," she sang. "Sit here. Sit here." The girl was too intent on her "child" to notice the mother's gasp as she ran to tell her husband, the chief. The chief called the girl's uncle and the two went to look behind the screen. Next to the bed they saw a huge white monster.

"Where did this come from?" the chief bellowed. But since the girl was still in seclusion, he had her mother question her. The girl told of finding the woodworm and taking it for a pet and finally of raising it as her child. The mother repeated the strange story to the chief.

"Now we know what it is that has been stealing the food! We must kill this strange creature." The chief called the men together.

"We have found the monster that has been eating our dried fish and grease," he told them. "My daughter has raised it from a woodworm. We must kill it before it kills all of us."

The men were amazed that such a thing could happen, but they set about making long wooden spears and hardening their points in the fire. Then they had to wait until the girl left her place of confinement.

The mother tried to coax the girl away from her pet. "Your confinement is over now," she told her. "Come, let's go help your aunt with her sewing."

THE GIRL AND THE WOODWORM

Although the girl loved this aunt dearly, she would not leave her pet. She suspected her secret had been found out, and was afraid something would happen to the woodworm while she was gone. There was no place to hide it, now that it had grown so large.

"Son, I have had a very bad dream," she told the worm one morning. "They have been begging me to come out, but how can I leave you? You have been my only company during my long and lonely confinement." She took the head of the woodworm, now too large to sit in her lap, and held it to her breast as she sang a lullaby to it. Her heart was full of sorrow, and tears ran down her cheeks.

Soon she heard the voice of her mother, speaking from behind the screen. "Come, let us go now to your aunt's house. You can now put on the fine marten robe she has sewn for your coming out ceremony," her mother said. "Soon you will be presented for marriage."

The girl laid the head of her sleeping "child" on the bed and went with her mother to her aunt's place. With a heavy heart she put on the marten robe. Then as she put the belt around her waist, she sang, "I have come out at last. You have begged me so hard. But it is like begging me to die. Leaving my pet will cause me to die."

She was unsteady in her walk, for her legs were weak from lack of exercise. Her chalk-white skin, almost transparent from the long fast and confinement, gave her an otherworldly appearance. She wept while she sang, and the people wept with her. They understood her sadness and admired her devotion. They also felt that she must have been given special powers, to have been able to raise a tiny woodworm into a monster. And in their love for her, they regretted that she must lose a companion she loved.

Then they all heard a terrible uproar. The

men were attacking the woodworm with their spears.

"They are killing my child!" she cried out to her uncle and his wife, the aunt who had sewn the marten robe for her.

"No, that's just a dogfight," said the uncle.

"They are killing him! They are killing my child!" she wailed. The uproar went on for a long time, for the monster put up a gallant fight. Finally everything grew still.

"They have killed you, my son! They got me away from you and killed you. It was not my fault."

Then she said to the people, "Let my son's body be burned in a huge wood fire. Let everyone in the town cut wood for it." The people, in awe of her powers, obeyed her and burned the body of her son with honor.

For the days and weeks that followed, the girl refused to eat or sleep. She sang her songs endlessly. Finally she, too, died and her people moved away from the village. But they remembered her devotion to her "child" and in her honor they took the Woodworm for their crest.

GUNARH-NESEGMET

Gunarh, like the Greek Orpheus, is a folk hero who loses his beloved wife and goes down to the underworld to find and rescue her. Orpheus wins the conditional release of Eurydice by playing enchantingly on his lyre, but he loses her again because he can't resist his desire to look at her before they reach the upper world.

Gunarh succeeds. On his way to the underworld home of the Blackfish, he helps the enslaved geese and woodcutter. They, in turn, help him outwit the Blackfish, rescue his wife and bring her safely home.

99

There was much excitement in the village the day the beautiful white sea otter floated into the bay in front of the beach. Canoes were lined up along the beachfront to get ready for the big seal hunt. Women were carrying baskets of food to store in the canoes and others were filling tightly woven baskets with stream water. The men were cleaning and repairing their weapons and getting their other things ready for the hunt.

The lovely young wife of Gunarh had just set down her basket when she noticed a commotion farther down the beach. Somebody had spotted the white sea otter and men were running to kill it. The beautiful fur caught her eye.

"Don't ruin the fur," she called to them. "Shoot it in the tail." As the chief's daughter she was used to giving orders and having them obeyed.

The men did as she told them and dragged the sea otter up to the beach, where they skinned it very carefully. Even so, when they spread it out on the beach, she noticed blood stains on the fur. She slid the pelt into the salt water at the water's edge to rinse it.

"This will make a beautiful robe," she said. "Or maybe we can hang it on the wall as a decoration." Gunarh watched her awhile, pleased to see her so happy with the fur, and then joined the other men to clean his weapons and tools.

The chief's daughter had been given to him in marriage as a reward for providing the village with so many seals. He had come here from another village after his father's death. This was the village of his mother's oldest brother, the uncle who, according to Native custom, would see to his upbringing and education.

Before his death, Gunarh's father had sent for him.

"My powerful club will now be yours, my son," the dying man had said. "Take good care of it, for it will prove useful to you. By its special powers it will gain you many seals. But be careful that no human beings see you use it. Have them hide their faces inside the canoe, and turn your face away after you float it out." He was referring to floating the club toward a group of seals, which it would mysteriously kill and bring back to the boat with it. This spirit club had been a gift to Gunarh's father for having paid proper respect to a sea anemone that others in the crew had ridiculed.

"I will do as you say, Father," Gunarh replied.

After the grieving period he and his mother set out for the uncle's village. The uncle received them cordially. He noticed how thin the boy was.

"You are going to need a little building up," he said. "Good food and hard exercise should take care of that."

It wasn't long before Gunarh was sitting in the icy water with three of his young cousins to build his endurance. Afterward they would switch one another with hemlock branches to toughen their skin and make the blood circulate. All of the high-class young men followed these rituals each morning. The rest of the day the four young boys spent doing chores and helping the canoe-builders. The four were inseparable.

"Is there a good tree near here for making a canoe?" Gunarh asked the other boys one night. "I can make a canoe."

They were surprised by this idea. It had not occurred to them to try to make a canoe by themselves. They had been only helpers on their various uncles' canoes. But so had he.

"What makes you think you can build a canoe?" one asked.

"I'm sure I could if I could find the right tree."

"There's one not far away that should make a fine canoe," volunteered one boy. The idea of making their own canoe appealed to him.

"Let's go get it," said Gunarh.

Early the next morning the boys got ready to go into the woods.

"Don't worry if we're not back tonight," Gunarh told his mother. "It may take us several days to find the right tree." Then he took his club from its safekeeping place and set out with it over his shoulder. The other boys carried adzes and a hammer and wedge.

They hiked through woods under tall hemlocks, spruce and, occasionally, cedar trees. Alder cropped up where trees had been cut down, but the slower-growing evergreens eventually crowded them out. In the meantime the alder made good firewood. The boys pushed through the berry bushes and devil's club and felt the spongy muskeg underfoot. They were looking for a tall cedar, one without lower branches to spoil the wood grain of the trunk. Its softer wood was easier to carve than spruce or hemlock, and its oil preserved the wood.

It was midmorning when they found the tree the boy had in mind. After inspecting it from all sides, they decided it was right for their canoe. They remembered to cut away a circle of bark and make cuts at the proper angles. Then taking turns with the hammer and wedge, they finally brought the tree down. After cutting off the top where the branches began, they started to shape the trunk.

Several days went by as the boys worked at shaping the canoe bottom with their adzes. Then they cut a little away from the other side before putting it over a fire to speed up the work of hollowing it. While the wood was slowly charring, they walked down to the water.

"Look at the seal out there!" said one of the boys.

"He's a big one. I'll get my club," Gunarh said.

The boys lay on the ground with their faces down. Then Gunarh floated the club out toward the seal and joined them on the ground.

"Do you think it will work?" one asked.

"I'll look in a few minutes," said Gunarh.

After a while Gunarh looked just to the water's edge to see whether the club had returned. There it was, with a freshly killed seal. It was quite a struggle for the boys to skin and cut up the seal, but they managed it. They prepared themselves a meal and hiked back to the village with the rest of the meat. When Gunarh's mother gave the seal to the chief, he was pleased.

"You boys will make good seal hunters," he told them. The boys were happy to have pleased the chief, but Gunarh was in a hurry to get back to building the canoe. They went right back to the woods.

Shaping the canoe took many long hours, but several weeks later they were able to launch it and set out for home. Gunarh went first to his mother's house.

"Mother, the canoe is finished. Now I would

like to have our ancestral hat, and to take the name my father gave me: Gunarhnesegmet."

His mother looked at her son. He had grown big and strong in the months since they had arrived at the village, and his bearing had become more confident.

"Yes, it is time for you to wear your father's hat and to take the name he gave you. You are a man now."

She brought out the hat she had carefully put away and gave it to him. Then he left with the other boys in the canoe. They set out first to catch some seals. When they came upon some around a huge rock, Gunarh floated his club toward them. He did this several times and each time it brought back a freshly killed seal. Each time, of course, he and the boys hid their faces. When they had all the seals they could handle, they headed for the village. He gave each boy a seal and then went to present the rest to his uncle. As the canoe approached the beach with its heavy load, the uncle noticed it.

"A strange canoe has come in with four people in it. It seems to have a big load." He did not recognize Gunarh and the boys at a distance. But the mother recognized the ancestral hat.

"That's my son and his friends."

"Your son! Ha! Where would he get a canoe? He's just a boy. And how could they catch such a big load of fish?"

But when the boat landed and the boys presented him with the seal, he was flabbergasted. He looked with amazement at Gunarh. His nephew looked so noble in his ancestral hat and his bearing had become so aristocratic. He looked so much bigger and stronger. His uncle realized that Gunarh had become a man.

"It is time you took the name your father left

you. From now on your tribal name will be
Gunarhnesegmet. You have built a sturdy canoe and
have proven yourself a fine hunter of seals. You will
bring great honor to our tribe."

Gunarh was much pleased at his uncle's
words. He would now be a full-fledged member of the
tribe and have a place of honor at gatherings. But his
uncle had not yet finished.

"It is you whom I choose to be my daughter's
husband." Gunarh could not believe it! The chief's
daughter was the most prized bride in the village. He
had often eyed the lovely girl with longing. But others
who were seeking her hand had better prospects. The
uncle had not really considered Gunarh before. He
thought of the men who were bigger and stronger and
seemed more likely to become leaders. He had not
noticed until today how fast Gunarh had been
developing.

"This is a great honor you bestow on me,
Uncle. I shall always prize your daughter and guard
her from harm." And though she had no say in the
matter, the chief's daughter was happy to have
such a handsome man of such high standing as her
husband.

Gunarh was thinking of that day and his
good fortune as he and the men cleaned their tools and
weapons after having killed and skinned the beautiful
white sea otter. His hunting skills had brought him
wealth and honor in the village, and his spirited little
wife was a real joy. He delighted in pleasing her.

His task done, he looked about for his wife.
Where was she? She was not in the shallow water.
What had happened to the sea-otter pelt? He went over
to the women at the water's edge. They were all staring
far out on the water. Then one noticed him there.

"Oh, Gunarh, a terrible thing has happened,"
she cried. "A huge blackfish has captured your wife."

"My wife captured? She couldn't be. I was right here."

"She was washing the sea-otter pelt and it started floating away," another woman said. "She kept wading after it, and when she was up to her waist in water, a huge blackfish sprang up and grabbed her."

"Did she drown?" the distraught Gunarh asked.

"No. We could hear her crying for help and she was holding on to its dorsal fin as the blackfish dived and surfaced."

Gunarh ran up to the communal house to consult the seer. But the women went on gossiping among themselves.

"Maybe she did something that is taboo," said one woman. "You know how casual she was about the taboos." The people knew they must be careful not to offend the creature that had been killed, and treat the body and pelt with respect. There were also certain actions they were to perform and others they were to avoid. Had Gunarh's wife been careless?

"Maybe the Sea People are unhappy that we have taken so many seal," said another. Although the people enjoyed the big catches Gunarh provided, they occasionally worried that they might be taking more than they really needed. Doing so could bring punishment.

In the community house the seer was listening to Gunarh's tale. When he finished, the seer spoke.

"The Killer Whale has captured your wife and taken her to his kingdom under the sea. She will live there now." Gunarh cried out in grief. This meant she had gone to another life.

"I'll go after her. How can I get to the Killer Whale kingdom?"

"No one has ever gone there and returned."

But the distraught Gunarh insisted.

"I will tell you as much as I know," the seer said. "First you have to find the place in the ocean that is above the entry to their kingdom below the water. Two kelp heads mark the spot. Swallow and Marten can guide you in the right direction. When you arrive there, tie your canoe to the kelp heads and then descend the kelp strands."

Gunarh thanked the seer and ran toward the door.

"Be sure to sing a chant to the Sea People while you journey, in case you have offended them." The seer too was worried about Gunarh's heavy catches of seal.

Gunarh called Swallow and Marten to him and they pushed off in the canoe. Marten sat forward in the bow to smell the trail. Swallow flew overhead to seek out the way. As they journeyed, Gunarh sang a chant to the sea creatures as the seer had directed. Once out in the ocean, he looked intently for signs of the blackfish. Finally in the distance he could make out a huge fish diving and surfacing. As he got closer, he could see someone clinging to the whale's dorsal fin.

"Save me! Oh, save me, my people!" It was his wife's voice!

Gunarh paddled vigorously to keep up with the blackfish. It was all he could do to keep it in sight as it cavorted in the water. Then suddenly it went into a deep dive and did not resurface. Gunarh paddled even harder until he reached the spot where the fish had disappeared. He noticed Swallow circling overhead. Then he saw the two kelp heads.

"This must be the place above the entry to the Killer Whale kingdom," he said to Marten. He began to tie his canoe to the kelp heads.

"Now you must go on alone," said Marten. "I will tend the canoe while Swallow returns to the village to tell them you are setting out to the dominion of the Killer Whale under the sea."

Gunarh did not find it strange that Marten spoke his language. Birds, fish and animals often took on the traits of people, and people could sometimes take on their traits. As he picked up his tools and got ready to go below the sea, an eerie feeling came over him. What would it be like in that underworld? He had swum underwater before, of course, but he had never gone to the ocean floor. The change to his uncle's village had been hard for him as a stranger, but those people would not have harmed him. What would these creatures be like? Would they be hostile? After all, he was coming to rescue his wife. And he did not know the terrain. He could be in danger.

But Gunarh could not spend much time with these thoughts. He had a big job ahead of him. He went over the side of the boat by the kelp heads and then lowered himself along their strands toward the ocean floor. The water was murky and he could see no lodgings or trails. He did not even know what these should look like in the world under the sea. As he got near the bottom, he saw something that looked like worms milling around.

"Hello! Here comes Gunarh for his wife," they cried. "We smell him."

As he got nearer, he saw that they were geese digging for roots. And they were blind! With his sharp knife he slit the skin over their eyes.

"There now! You can see!" They gabbled and paddled around and dug among the roots.

"Do you know the way to the Killer Whale kingdom?" he asked.

"You can go this way. But be careful. If they catch you, you will never get away alive." They also showed him a different way to go back if he was being followed.

He took the first trail they had pointed out. The way was rocky at first, but when he had gone some distance, it began to look like a trail through the woods. There were trees all about and he felt the muskeg beneath his feet. Then he heard someone cutting wood. But before he came to the woodsman, the chopping stopped. Then he saw the woodsman sitting on a log, looking very unhappy.

"I have broken my wedge," he explained. "My Killer Whale master will be angry if I bring such a small load of wood."

"I can fix your wedge if you will help me find my wife. The Killer Whale has captured her." Gunarh was sure the woodsman would agree to help. He would be grateful for the favor, of course, but that was not the main reason. He was from another tribe, forced to do menial work. He would be pleased at the chance to play a trick on his master.

"You must be Gunarh. I'll do whatever I can to help. In fact, this wood is for your wife."

"She is still alive, then?"

"Oh yes. The chief has claimed her for his wife and wants to put a black fin on her back. They are building a fire now to char the wood."

Gunarh groaned. "Not my wife's back! Not while I live!" He took the parts of the wedge and put them up to his mouth to wet them, stuck them together, and then blew on the wedge. The two parts held and he gave the repaired tool back to the woodcutter. As he went back to chopping wood, the two came up with a plan for rescuing Gunarh's wife. The woodsman was sure he could persuade other slaves, his fellow tribesmen, to help him.

When the wood made a large enough load, the woodsman picked it up and led the way to the house. Gunarh followed, staying out of sight among the trees. When they arrived, Gunarh was surprised to see a longhouse similar to those in his village, but much larger. The outside planking was painted with a killer whale design, and the tall totem running up the middle of the front had an opening that served as the door.

Since nobody was in sight, Gunarh went up to the door and peered in. He saw Killer Whales seated on the tiers around the fire, which was in the center. They looked like ordinary people, only much larger. Then his heart leaped as he saw his wife warming herself at the fire, her back toward him. He wanted to run to her. But that would have been foolish. The Killer Whales would have captured him easily. The woodcutter's plan called for him to stay outside while he and his friends prepared the way.

"Hey, Gitska," the woodcutter called to one of the slaves. "Where are you going with that water?"

"I am going to hang it over the fire to heat."

"Good. When I give the signal, upset it over the rocks."

Gitska looked puzzled. Ordinarily the hot rocks were put into the kettle to heat the water. The woodcutter told him of the rescue plan. The slave, a fellow tribesman, was happy to help.

Gunarh waited just inside the door in a spot not lighted by the fire. He kept his eyes on his wife. Quite a group had assembled by now. When the chief began to address the people, the woodcutter gave his signal. The slave, who had been walking around the fire, tripped and fell against the hanging basket, spilling the water over the hot rocks. A cloud of steam rose all around them. In the confusion Gunarh ran over and grabbed his wife.

"Come with me! Quick!"

She pulled away from the strong arm holding her.

"Who are you? What do you want?"

"It's Gunarh, your husband. We have to run."

She recognized his voice and realized he had come for her.

"How did you get here?"

"I'll tell you later. Run!"

They dashed through the door where the woodcutter was.

"Here, eat this quickly," Gunarh said, stuffing a tobacco-like powder into the woodcutter's mouth. Immediately the woodcutter's body began to swell.

When the mist cleared, the Killer Whales saw that Gunarh's wife was gone. They rushed for the door, but the woodcutter's large body blocked the way. The women sprayed him with water to make him shrink, but he shrank very slowly. By the time they could get through the door, Gunarh and his wife were far ahead on the trail. The Killer Whale people dashed after them and were gaining on them as they approached the home of the geese whose sight Gunarh had restored.

"Run, Prince, run!" the geese shouted. "We'll save you," and sent them along the alternate trail they had pointed out earlier. After Gunarh had left them the first time, they had busied themselves setting traps along the main trail to trick anyone who might chase the couple on their return. As they expected, the Killer Whales showed up.

"Where did they go?" the Killer Whales asked as they got close to the geese.

"This way," they said, luring them to the trail with the traps. Meanwhile Gunarh and his wife kept running until they reached the spot below the canoe. Gunarh lifted his wife and together they shinnied up the kelp strands. Marten was in the canoe to give them a hand when they reached the top.

Once in the boat, Gunarh's wife paddled along with him. They were almost home when they saw the blackfish behind them again. Even with the two paddling at full strength the fish were gaining on them. Then they noticed a large, double-finned blackfish in the lead. He was zigzagging in front of the others to keep them from reaching the fleeing couple.

"I am the woodcutter," the double-finned fish called out to them. "From now on you will know me from the other blackfish by my two fins." Their friend had helped them again.

Gunarh and his wife reached the bay of their village exhausted. The people were happy to see them. They had missed Gunarh, the seal hunter, for their provisions were running low. The tales of their adventures in the underworld amazed and entertained the people for many nights of storytelling.

R E L A T E D   R E A D I N G

Barbeau, Marius. *Haida Myths*. Ottawa: National Museum of Canada, 1953.

——. *Totem Poles I & II*. Ottawa: National Museum of Canada.

Garfield, Viola, and Linn Forest. *The Wolf and the Raven: Totem Poles of Southeast Alaska*. Seattle: University of Washington Press, 1956.

Keithahn, Edward. *Monuments in Cedar*. Seattle: Superior Publishing Company, 1963.

Krause, Aurel. *The Tlingit Indians*. Translated by Erna Gunther. Seattle: University of Washington Press, 1958.

Laguna, Frederica de. *Under Mount St. Elias: The History and Culture of the Yakutat Indians*. Washington, D.C.: Smithsonian Institution Press, 1972.

Oberg, Kalvero. *The Social Economy of the Tlingit Indians*. Seattle: University of Washington Press, 1973.

Olson, Ronald L.: *Social Structure and Social Life of the Tlingit in Alaska*. Anthropological Records, Vol. 26. Berkeley: University of California Press, 1967.

Swanton, John R. *Haida Texts and Myths*. Washington, D.C.: Johnson Reprint Corporation, 1970.

——. *Social Conditions, Beliefs, and Linguistic Relationship of the Tlingit Indians*. Washington, D.C.: Johnson Reprint Corporation, 1970.

——. *Tlingit Myths and Texts*. Washington, D.C.: Johnson Reprint Corporation, 1970.

ABOUT THE AUTHOR

Mary L. Beck is a classical scholar (M.A. from Stanford) who has lived in Ketchikan, Alaska, since 1951, when she married a third-generation Alaskan. Besides rearing a family, she taught literature and writing courses for thirty years at Ketchikan Community College, a branch of the University of Alaska. Mary has an abiding interest in the Native culture of Southeast Alaska and a commitment to recording its rich oral literature. *Heroes and Heroines in Tlingit-Haida Legend* is her first book.

Many books on Native heritage are available from Alaska Northwest Books™. Ask at your favorite bookstore or write us for a free catalog.

Alaska Northwest Books™
A division of GTE Discovery Publications, Inc.

P.O. Box 3007
Bothell, WA 98041-3007
(206) 487-6100
Toll free 1-800-343-4567